PRAISE FOR
Katie Rodriguez Banister's On A Roll

"I love the honesty."

— **Tina Christanell,**
Counselor, Sperring Middle School

"Katie has been through a tremendous amount of adversity yet found a real calling. It is evident through this book how one can become truly comfortable in their own skin, even if their sensation is limited! Katie's Coping Strategies should be on the wall in every Spinal Cord Injury unit. This book is highly relatable regardless of disability status. However, for those who have experienced SCI, it is a must-read. They should give out this book on all SCI floors so family, friends, and persons with SCI can read it or have it read to them as they are ready. I plan to have my OT students read it to better understand a personal perspective on SCI. While not everyone who reads this book will have a spinal cord injury or even know someone with one, they will relate to the humanity of Katie's memoir."

— **Dr. Carla Walker, Advance Practice Clinician,**
Washington University School of Medicine Program
in Occupational Therapy

"Heartfelt, funny, educational and brutally honest. From family dynamics to the accident, rehab, bladder management and dating, a real love story and spiritual journey."

— **JET, The Expert, Book Reviewer**

"On A Roll was very inspirational!! It gave me hope with my current physical limitations due to an automobile accident. I realize that the feelings and thoughts that I have are normal and expected. But now, I feel that I can still be everything that I want to be and more..."

— Burchell McGhee, Avid Reader

"The description of the court case was riveting and chilling. So interesting to read the play by play."

— Daryle Glynn Brown, News Producer

"On A Roll is powerful and horrifying and beautiful. ---Like driving past an accident scene---we know we should not stop and stare, but we cannot help it. While Katie doesn't leave the reader with a wish of "Oh I would love to have her life and her chair," she does help us to understand that her life didn't end when she got injured. Katie answers questions people have about being in a wheelchair but are too embarrassed to ask! She even tells us, without shame, about emptying the bladder and having sex."

**— LC Van Savage Author,
Columnist and Television Host, Brunswick, Maine**

"Katie shares her stories and experiences in such a way that connects with anyone as a presenter and in her memoir. Well done!"

**— Jason Ayran, Workforce Development Manager,
Saint Louis Zoo**

"I could feel your personality and it seemed like I was having a conversation with you. It was well done and a fun read! Your positivity and enthusiasm are infectious and inspiring."

**— Aaron Swatosh MS,
Professional School Counselor**

On A Roll

How It Feels
To Be On Wheels

On A Roll

How It Feels
To Be On Wheels

KATIE RODRIGUEZ BANISTER

with Jo Lena Johnson and
Andrew Szanton

Access-4-All, LLC

Access-4-All, LLC
PO Box 220751
St. Louis, MO 63122-0751

Contact the Author at: KatieRBanister@Outlook.com

Book Interior and E-book Design by Amit Dey | amitdey2528@gmail.com

AWomanOnWheels.com

ISBN 978-0-9744908-6-1

My birth family got me here.
My soul family keeps me here.

Foreword

(Katie as Rosie in "Bye Bye Birdie," 1983)

Why would Katie Rodriguez Banister write a memoir when she's only in her early 50s? The answer is because she has quite a story to tell.

When I met Katie, she was 17 years old: perky, funny, cute, flirty, and the life of the party! She auditioned for my dance team that entertained at half-times of our high school's home football and basketball games. Of course, she made the squad. She was quite a dancer --- and a singer, too. So, she and I also worked together when she was in the school's Show Choir and when she had leads in "Oklahoma" and "Bye Bye Birdie," the school's Broadway musicals for two consecutive years. (I was the choreographer for the high school.) She had even been her community's Junior Miss. Yes, Katie was — and is — adorable.

We lost touch after she graduated high school, but I knew she was still active in college, majoring in Recreation and Business Management. After college, just for fun, she also taught aerobics. Then the rollover accident happened, and Katie's life was changed forever. I visited Katie in the hospital with a colleague who had been the vocal music director at our high school, and we held our tears until we got to the elevator after leaving Katie's room. That visit was in the early recovery days for Katie when she was still wearing what is called a "halo" (which will be explained in her memoir). We couldn't get over — and I still can't — Katie's positive and optimistic attitude, along with her acceptance of what would be her new reality. Katie had become a quadriplegic, paralyzed from the chest down. Through the years she has thrived by finding her loving husband, seeking out various life philosophies, and sharing her story with audiences who benefit greatly from her speaking engagements.

You will read her story in her own voice and you will be moved by the honesty and depth of her words. And guess what?! She is still perky, funny, cute, flirty, and the life of the party — even as a Woman on Wheels.

Penny Stein, Katie's Pom Pom Coach
Kirkwood High School English Department (1972-1999)

Contents

Acknowledgements

Steven Louis Banister, you are the love of my life. My God, I never thought I would ever find the absolute perfect match to me, yet here you are! Our marriage and life together are better than I could have ever imagined – with or without wheels, thank you.

Thanks to my family, especially my siblings, for the years of love, growth and being the wonderful, supportive and caring souls, you are. I love and appreciate you dearly.

I am grateful to several special, super helpful beings for assisting me during the writing of this book. Thank you Phyllis Banister, Franklin and Tresa McCallie, LC Van Savage, Kyla Chambers and Carla Walker.

To my caregivers. You show up. You get me showered, dressed and busy in my office. Your hands are mine every morning and I am very grateful, thank you.

Many *Oprah* magazine articles influenced my ideas about happiness. Ms. Winfrey, thank you for the wonderful work you do and the huge difference you make in people's lives – and especially mine!

Last, but definitely not least, thank you God. Because I know you're here, there and everywhere.

My Co-Writers

I met Jo Lena Johnson in 2019 at a St. Louis Publishers Association meeting. The way she ran the meeting was dynamic. When I saw her in action, I knew I had to work with her. She is a book coach, publisher and writer but another part of her mission is helping authors fully express their message, experience growth and get a better understanding of themselves. Jo Lena pulled more out of me than a phlebotomist!

Andrew Szanton is a memoir writer who lives in Newton, Massachusetts, just west of Boston and he helped me tell my story with words I could have never created on my own. I am so grateful for our mutual St. Louis friend, Loretta Haggard, who introduced us.

Introduction

Have you ever felt like life was out of control? Or that you were trapped in a situation or circumstance from which you couldn't escape? Have you done all you could to change things, but realized certain situations were beyond your control? Have you been tempted to give up, lose hope or stop standing up for yourself, for your loved ones, or for your strength and success? If yes, you're not alone.

We're all going through something.

I'm here to tell you, you can survive!

I was living life and doing the best I could, but being the sixth child of seven, along with my dad issues made it difficult. I was a creative type who loved performing, it was a way to express myself, and to also cope with life. I went to college and majored in Recreation. Of course, I wanted love like most young women, so dating was also a priority at that time. I struggled a bit but was optimistic about having a bright future.

In 1990, at 25 years old, I was in an auto accident and became a quadriplegic.

That wasn't in my plan.

Discovering I would spend the rest of my life using a wheelchair and dealing with the realities of how that would affect my life put me in a tailspin for a while. I spent so much time battling emotions, thoughts and discovering the therapy I would need to live this new life, **On A Roll**.

I was so controlling and angry. Something had to change.

Since I couldn't force my body to walk or function as it did before the accident, I focused my mind to cooperate with the parts of my body I could still use to live in this new reality. It took time, practice, patience, working through depression, and learning how to let go of that anger. As a child my Dad was tough, yet, as an adult, he was who I needed, and thankfully, our relationship got better with time.

As if fighting for my life wasn't enough, there were extremely difficult years of The Car Company trying to blame/shame me for being in *their* faulty vehicle! I met a man named Steve while I was advocating for justice, who eventually became my loving and devoted husband. With the support, love and desire to do more than simply survive, I learned ways to cope and thrive.

It's been 30 years since my accident and I'm sharing *How It Feels to Be On Wheels* because I want you to know that whatever you're dealing with, you've got this!

I promise you an honest look at anger and finding healthy ways to move through it and past it. My depression never fully goes away, but I share my journey as an example of possibilities.

Humor, laughing and finding the fun in life will help you on a daily basis. I'm living proof.

It may take time, patience and understanding as you work through it, but I have faith in you, and you should too!

PART ONE

Finding My Groove

I was young and strong, outgoing, petite, having fun and in the prime of my life... Though I wanted a man, I was in my own way, so I chose therapy.

Life's going to only get better from here, right?

My First Time On Wheels

It's ironic that I had chosen a wheelchair as part
of a college class project in 1986.

y mind would go back in time and pick on parts of the past which I saw differently now. In college, I had majored in Recreation. "You're majoring in fun!" my family teased me, but it wasn't all fun and games. I took a class in 1987 called "Special Populations." To help learn to understand people with disabilities, everyone had to choose a disability for a day. I chose being in a manual wheelchair, in one I had to physically push. It was an "adult large" chair, so self-pushing was very difficult with my petite frame.

My good friend and suite mate Toni was my "aide" for the day.

This was new to me; I hadn't gone to school with kids with disabilities. In the 1970s, St. Louis had a special school district for children with disabilities like autism, Down Syndrome, vision or hearing challenges, as well as physical disabilities.

In just that one day I learned a lot: Going through a cafeteria line in a wheelchair was a pain because I needed help to get everything and I couldn't reach my own tray. I felt helpless. It was also hard trying to roll through the heavy doors of each academic building constructed before they had electric doors. Most of the water fountains on campus were suddenly inaccessible to me.

The campus, once small to me, now seemed big and spacious, and I felt tiny and unable to independently navigate the wheelchair. The quadrangle at the heart of campus seemed twice as big and it took forever to get anywhere.

Most of all, I learned that people stare at you if you're in a wheelchair, and it feels belittling. You can't tell if they *intend* to belittle you or not, but when it happens repeatedly, it's offensive, regardless of the intent. *Oh, well,* I thought, *At least I'm only disabled for one day.*

At the end of the day, Toni was pushing me back to the dorms, but stopped to talk to someone. She left my wheelchair on a small incline, and my wheelchair and I started rolling down the hill.

My books fell out of my lap, the wheelchair was out of control, and so -- just as two guys who didn't know me came running over to help -- I tumbled out of the wheelchair as it continued to roll down the hill. Then I stood straight up.

Staying in character, Toni screamed, "It's a miracle!"

I laughed, Toni laughed and eventually so did the two guys who'd come running to help.

You never know what life will throw your way.
Truth is stranger than fiction...

This Wasn't My Vision, But It Is My Life

I'm a woman on wheels, a chick in a chair and a living example that life isn't fair.

I'm a St. Louis girl who was paralyzed in a car accident in 1990 and has lived using a wheelchair ever since. It's been tough in a lot of ways, but I want no pity. When I make a mistake, I try again with a lot of help from others and a great husband. I live a good life.

Anger is Natural

I don't like being angry, but it is in my blood. I feel I've come full circle though. At dinner this past Thanksgiving, I confronted my family and shared my feelings. I found them to be accepting and I got hugs from those who had also harbored layers of anger.

Anger, as a constant, does no one any good. Anger can fuel creativity, by turning anger into art, but letting it fester, and rage, burns everything and everyone along the path. Letting anger go is essential to finding peace.

Blessed are the Peacemakers

My nature is peaceful and fair, and I actually crave harmony and connection with people, like most Libras. Yet, I was raised in a large super-competitive family, which could be intimidating, as I found it difficult to find my place and let my voice be heard. Growing up, I often kept things in just to keep the peace.

The blessing of my wheelchair gives me a little extra room to be outrageous. I often say things that others are thinking but don't dare say. I think there's value in that. I'll admit, in some situations, a tactful silence is the best policy and at times, my blunt honesty has gotten me in trouble. But I rarely regret it because being outspoken is the way I am.

When Bad Things Happen

Bad things happen and the only real control we have is our reaction to them. When something bad happens, be with it. What does be with it mean? Get through your emotions by acknowledging them, experiencing them, and mourning your losses – allowing yourself to face what you're feeling. They are real and if you need to process your feelings about your situation, ask for help from a trusted resource.

One time I called the suicide hotline and it helped to talk to a compassionate person.

Also, you can center yourself by focusing on your breath. Inhale and exhale slowly to help stop the racing thinking. Take a couple more breaths, grab a pen and paper, and work on a plan to deal with what you've been dealt. Depression and anxiety never fully go away, but with practice they can become easier to manage.

We Live Our Lives and Sometimes Suffer Tragedies

My car accident, and the reality of my life since then, didn't take away my optimism. I still have a deep love for life. I crave happiness, I need joy and my favorite t-shirt says, "Fun must be the most important dis- cipline of all."

I have had 25 years to lead a very physical life, and 30 years to think things over. It's interesting to me that we all play stories in our minds and, over time, those stories become our truths. There is no single truth about "what happened" in the world, just all of these stories play- ing in our heads, often inherited from our parents and passed down to our children.

I'm not immune from this process, of creating a world from my own stories and calling it "what happened." Still, I've tried to be conscious of how this works, and to reach out to other people, other cultures, other faiths to hear their stories, and to braid them into my own.

I believe we're all put on this earth for some reason. In my case, the reason was to help other people learn. My teaching is not done as long as the little child in the grocery store sees a person with a disability and gets shushed by the adult with them. We need to talk to each other, ask questions in kind ways to learn about each other and find more joy in life. When we learn, we grow.

Hot Girl

At 25 years old I was short tempered and didn't have
a pause button at all.

*M*y sister had given me a copy of the book *Our Bodies, Ourselves*. For several years, I'd been using dating and sex to try to find happiness. I'd had no trouble finding willing partners. I figured God gave us our sexuality to be enjoyed, right? Wearing a white polo shirt and a blue jean mini-skirt, bobby socks and tennis shoes, I was sexy and confident, knowing I looked good. But this image and hot girl behavior came at a price because on the inside, I wasn't happy. I was unable to fix or find what was missing, like many of us in our mid-20's.

It was a hot summer day in St. Louis, in 1989. My younger brother Tom and I were settled into our new apartment. I put on my one-piece hot pink leopard print swimsuit, grabbed a boom-box and a beach towel, and headed over to the complex's pool…

All the lounge chairs were empty on the top tier surrounding the pool. I flipped my Tone Loc cassette into my player and closed my eyes. The sun melted my muscles and I toe-tapped to the tune, "Wild Thing."

A few minutes later, a very tall young lady in a neon green two-piece swimming suit asked me, "Hi, is this lounge chair open?"

I said, "It's yours for the taking."

She put her stuff down and stretched out on the chair. She had long legs that didn't quit.

"Hi, my name is Katie."

"Hey, I'm Delilah," she said, slathering on her tanning lotion. "I live just three buildings over."

"Me, too!"

We got to talking and laughed at the same things, finding much in common. Soon Delilah and I were hanging out together almost every night. She was 23 and I was 25. She was over 6 feet tall, and I was just under 5 feet tall. We enjoyed going out together, dancing and looking for guys.

Our favorite club, now closed, was Impressions. It was a nice club, not too stuffy, a half-mile from our apartment, off Lemay Ferry Road and South Lindbergh. It had a bar, tables, and a deejay who played everything from Aerosmith to Donna Summer.

Delilah would sit, as she danced very rarely. We'd people-watch, make up stories about them and leave after an hour.

On my days off, I'd yell at the bottom of her window, "Hey, Delilah! Come over for breakfast!" We loved watching TV and movies together. But it was more than that. She was a friend -- someone I knew I could count on. She could count on me, too.

I would wear a skirt and heels in those days and get a lot of attention. I loved that, "click, click, click" sound as my four-inch purple pumps went walking down a hallway. I felt assured, like I was on my way to something important. But I could also tell that some people saw

11

me walking by and hated me. I could feel their negative energy, and it hurt. They looked at me and I knew they were thinking, "What a bitch!"

If only they could see me on the inside.

We unfairly judge ourselves and others consciously
and unconsciously every day.
We do it and we have to acknowledge it.
We should stop this.

Seeing A Therapist Helped

I wanted to get rid of pain and find peace.

In late 1989, I was 25 years old and realized I needed a therapist because I didn't have a healthy relationship with men, nor could I find a job in my chosen field, Recreation.

I was moving a little too fast in those days, more confident on the outside than the inside. I kept busy, met people, made my own personal greeting cards, wrote poetry, and stayed on the go. So why wasn't I happy? My life and my thoughts were not deep enough to fill me.

Twice a week, I started seeing a psychotherapist named Karen. We met through my parent's friends, who were both therapists. Karen was thin and pretty, with soft brown hair. She was gentle in her gestures and dressed more conservatively than I did. She looked "soft", but I soon discovered that Karen could be strong and stern. I liked her and was impressed with the balance.

In our first appointment, in November of 1989, while crying a river, I handed Karen a list of 30 things I felt I needed to accomplish in order to transform into a happier and successful person.

13

One of the areas I needed to work on was my reaction to those older than me. I wanted to stop feeling intimidated or insecure whenever someone in my family or at work said something that I disagreed with. I didn't want to be bitter, angry or an unhappy employee.

Looking at this long list of goals, Karen took a breath and said, "Well, we better get busy." She had eyes which showed me honesty and sincerity. She wasn't going to try to be funny because she knew I needed real help. She could tell I was a doer and wanted to do something about the way I was feeling. Karen was a doer, too.

Most of the items on my list were related to one primary issue: I wanted to learn how to develop and keep healthy relationships. I needed to stop hating my father and hating myself.

I wasn't going to settle and marry just anybody, but nice guys didn't have a chance around me. The older I got, and the more I saw friends getting married, the more frustrated I was with my dating life.

Karen was a great therapist, and for three straight weeks, twice a week, I cried like Niagara Falls.

Karen told me, "It's okay. You have some issues and together we're going to find out why. We need a game plan, but we can do this." I spoke out, feeling like a tennis player hitting some hard, flat shots whistling across the net. Every shot came back. This woman was always ready to play.

By the third and fourth month of therapy, I understood myself a little better, was finding inner peace and had more confidence. Growing up I had to hear, over and over from my father, "You're only #6, what do you know?" This caused me to dislike Dad for most of my childhood. Crying less and getting stronger, at 25 years old, I knew that I was more than, "Just kid #6" and I wasn't allowing myself to be subjected to others' judgement as I had in the past.

Honestly, therapy saved my life.

My Dark Secret

I tried to love my father, but at that time, I couldn't, I wasn't there yet. *This relationship was my focus in therapy* until a suppressed memory popped out of me during an early session. I was incredibly sad about my childhood, I told Karen what I'd meant to keep secret always: that I'd been repeatedly sexually molested, by a 16-year-old girl who lived close to my neighborhood when I was seven or eight years old.

My dark secret was out, and Karen assured me that none of what she did to me had been my fault. Hearing her say that helped me, as I began to forgive myself and much of that shame. I let go of a lot of pain, feeling relief from all of those things I had told myself.

Karen used to say, "Life is very beautiful, but trauma can keep us from seeing its full beauty."

What I learned was: A person who's been through trauma must first accept the need to grieve; and then to learn how to grieve. Once you've learned those two things, you're ready to move on to the beauty in life.

Whenever she repeated that I always replied, "I see the need to grieve but I don't have time to learn how to grieve!"

Karen would say calmly, "We will practice until you know how to grieve."

What I Learned About Counseling

Counseling will support you if you are willing to do the work. Facing your demons takes effort. You must face who you are; your warts and all. You'll learn why you are the way you are and if you want to change it up, counseling is the door to knock on. I also suggest you or a trusted person write some of your thoughts down and then bringing them to your sessions. It can help you start the conversation and/or keep you focused.

Therapy is a gift you give to yourself. I realized I didn't need to know about my therapist's life, I was there to work on me. Knowing this allowed me to relax and focus on improving my mental health. Learning to understand and love yourself enables others to do the same.

My Last Dance

I enjoyed the whole groove as I laughed and danced the night away!

One night, Delilah, her roommate Sharon and I were at the Broadway Oyster Bar, a little bar with dancing in downtown St. Louis, near Busch Stadium. The blues were playing, with a little funk and R&B sprinkled in. Everyone in the place was having fun. A gentleman in his 50's with gray hair and a genuine smile, approached me. He gave me a bow and cordially asked, "May I have this dance?"

"Sure!" I said.

He and I twirled all around the compact dance area. I laughed and had so much fun, I danced way more than I drank, and the band played on.

I didn't know it then, but that was my last dance.

My Life Rolled Over

I'm feeling empty inside with feelings I can't hide.
I have tried. But I just cry.

Change happens every day, to everyone. You can't stop it. On February 11, 1990, I awoke at 7:30 am and called my neighbor Delilah and her roommate Sharon. Just four days before, I had found the job of my dreams: a social director for an apartment community in St. Louis County. It was a full-time job, with benefits. I had a place to live, money in the bank.

It was unseasonably warm, maybe 75 degrees in St. Louis in February! I needed to go out and enjoy the beautiful day. We did just that, and spent the day in Hermann, a cute little river town about two hours away that's filled with antique dealers, wineries and breathtaking views of the Missouri River.

Delilah owned a small SUV made by a Car Company, and we took that because it had the most gas. Delilah drove. I put on my seatbelt, as I always did when riding in a car. We were laughing and having a great time, driving through the rolling hills. We sat down with some total strangers at lunch, and they turned out to be very nice people. Old friends and new friends, sunshine and great views. It had been a perfect day.

The new friends we'd met at lunch wanted to take us to another winery but suddenly, Delilah said, "Wait a minute, Katie, it's 4:30 and 'The Simpsons' are on in two hours."

"Oh, my God," I said. "You're right. We've got to go home."

We honked at our new friends and yelled, "We have to go home!" They waved goodbye.

The SUV had a wheelbase that was too narrow and a center of gravity that was too high. About 20 minutes into our drive home, at Marthasville, Missouri, the vehicle suddenly rolled over.

And my seatbelt failed.

It's difficult to describe what happened next, but I've been told that I really shouldn't have physically survived. Yet, I was paralyzed from the chest down.

In the Helicopter

A piercing siren was sounding. I was lying in a field of grass, I couldn't move, and I thought I might be dying. But instinct told me, *Katie, this isn't your day to check out.*

Then a paramedic was kneeling by my side, and I could hear a helicopter whipping its way toward me. The lips of the paramedic were moving, he was trying to tell me something, but the THUP-THUP-THUP of the helicopter blades drowned out everything else.

I was flown to Barnes Hospital in St. Louis. In the helicopter, male voices were all around me. It was a distortion, a blur. I was there, but not there… I just knew I wasn't ready to die.

I had no healthcare coverage. I had thought, *I'm young and healthy. Why should I be paying health care premiums for care I don't need?* I'd only been a hospital patient once before in my life, to get my tonsils out, at the age of 17 when I was on my parents' insurance plan. I'd never broken a bone in my life.

Now I was paralyzed.

Paralysis felt a little like stage fright, or butterflies before a presentation I had to make. But in the past, I'd overcome butterflies with a steady breath and resolve. I'd worked through them quickly and they'd gone away.

Paralysis was not going anywhere, and there was nothing I could do. I was not in control.

PART TWO

Shock to Anger to Gratitude

I was paralyzed.

*As I faded in and faded out, I let go of my thoughts
and held on to my faith in God.*

I knew that God knew, I wasn't ready to go.

That abnormally warm winter afternoon I fought for my life, and for the next few years I would fight a legal battle to prove that Delilah's SUV wasn't a safe vehicle.

Why did this happen to me??? I. Do. Not. Know.

Am I happy when things don't go the way I want them to?

No. I can feel my blood boiling at those times. I have endured, knowing that I have the ability to control my reactions. When life makes me mad, I recognize that and then find a way to make peace.

I am not bitter. On the other hand, my life isn't easy. I need help to empty my bladder, get dressed, eat, to do just about everything. My spontaneity is gone. However, my wheelchair has taught me about patience, caring, and making wise use of my time.

Over the years, through all types of therapy, endless days of rigorous focus, periods of tears and depression, and enormous amounts of love and support from those around me, I learned to cope.

The Intensity of Intensive Care

I've always been independent and in a hurry.
The accident changed everything.

Thank goodness I am not a quitter...

An older nurse rushed in, full of conviction and said, "Doctor, we have a young woman, MVA (Motor Vehicle Accident), just admitted. She's paralyzed from the chest down. Do you think we'll need to put her on a ventilator?"

I looked around the room and yelled, "Where in the hell am I? And where's my damn purse?"

The doctor said, "No need for a vent with this one. I think we have a bit of luck and a strong will here."

I looked around at the chaos. Beeps, tubes and x-ray machines. People in white everywhere and they wouldn't leave me alone.

A nurse was harassing me, "Katie, do you know where you are? Do you know what happened?"

"No, I don't!"

My body couldn't move but my mind was racing. *What just happened? What is happening now? When can I get out of here? This can't be happening -- it's not on my To Do list!*

It's in my DNA to get furious when I can't be in control of my life.

Everyone around me was busy, busy, busy, but it felt as if time had stopped.

Then I started begging, "Could someone get me out of here, please? I'm not supposed to be here. I've got too much to do!"

But no one answered.

I yelled, "This isn't fair! For God's sake... I'm a good person. Please God, I don't deserve this!"

A different nurse whipped out a needle, poked my IV drip and said in a calm manner, "Now, you just take it easy."

I wanted to yell, *Give me the list of my injuries! I'll deal with it!* But I was so shaken I'm not sure if I verbalized that or not.

In time, I learned what I had: A spinal cord badly injured at the C-5 and C-6 cervical vertebrae, plus a hairline fracture in my jaw, a crushed left shoulder blade, a fractured left hip, two fractured ribs, a punctured lung and a broken neck. I also had damage to my left kidney that, two years later, would lead to the laparoscopic removal of that kidney.

Oh, how I wanted to get out of Intensive Care, and move on to rehabilitation, I love exercise and looked forward to getting back to my action-packed life full of music and movement!

I sang and danced across the stage all throughout high school. My senior year I was voted "Most Likely to Win an Oscar" for my role as

Rosie Alvarez in the musical, "Bye Bye Birdie." I loved exercising and I'd been a heck of an aerobics teacher on land and in water during my entire, short, adult life. As I lay, watching the action around me, I wanted to choose more great music and make it fun.

But now I was sick and stuck in bed. Psychologically I was prepared to get moving again, but physically I was put on hold.

"Okay, Katie, let's take that temperature again," announced the charge nurse who was walking toward my hospital bed.

I replied, "I've gotta get out of here. No offense, but I'm sick of people coming and going while I'm stuck here like feathers on fresh tar. Please, please, *please*, give me a good temp, lady in white!"

She put the thermometer in my mouth and said politely, "Shhhhh."

I lay there for what seemed like an eternity until she finally removed the slender glass probe between my lips.

"Well?" I begged.

"Well, you're not going to like this," she replied.

"There is too much of what I don't like right now! Just tell me what my temperature is!" I demanded.

"Katie, you are still at 100 so we can't move you."

"100 is not so bad," I countered.

"Katie," she said, with her head tilted to the side.

This looked like judgment or pity, so I yelled, "This is bullshit!"

"And getting angry is not helping the cause," said the nurse.

Alone again, I lay in my bed crying. My temperature seemed to pulsate like a volcano. I said quietly, "Look, God, I want to advance myself. Go on to the next thing because I'm bored out of my gourd." I was so ready to get out of intensive care!

Spinal Fusion Surgery

I had to get through six hours of spinal fusion surgery to put the bones in my neck back together again. My heart ached, and my head hurt, and all I could do was look out my hospital window and hope the next temp taken would allow me to move on.

I was in shock; there were so many things I hadn't come to terms with yet. But through the haze of surgeries, fatigue and visitors there was one thing I knew; most of my options were gone. I felt like Dorothy in "The Wizard of Oz" movie when her house is carried off in a storm and her whole life trajectory is changed.

I thought, no *more high heels, no more bike rides and playing tennis on hot summer days. No more sex?! But yes, I would still have menstrual cycles and cramps. Does that suck, or what? God, why couldn't you paralyze my menstrual cramps?*

The life I had is no longer.

My diaphragm was paralyzed, which makes coughing difficult.

Quadriplegics can't warm or cool our bodies easily. Because of my injuries my body could no longer sweat. Anyone who has spent time in St. Louis during the summer will understand why that scared me.

It was even worse than I knew because the blood transfusion I'd been given had some blood in it contaminated with Hepatitis C. It was only two years later that blood banks would start testing donated blood for Hepatitis C. I wouldn't learn until many years later that I had the ailment, when medicine I was prescribed almost killed me.

All around me, I saw fellow patients who were simply existing, in despair. Sometimes I actually saw them in the process of giving in, surrendering to stillness. Lying around in bed, eating chips and candy bars, and resisting any kind of Rehab. The truth of the matter is, Rehab is hard. It's really hard work and while I understood why they felt like giving up, I wished I had the power to motivate and save us all.

Delusions

The pain meds and their effects were horrific...

Those first few weeks were strange and awful. I was traumatized from the accident itself. And couldn't rest, with the sounds of the machines, constantly interrupting my sleep. I began to lose track of space and time as the past and present comingled in my mind. For instance, I began obsessing over seeing my first dead body. It was great aunt Marge's husband, my great uncle Gene, who'd been laid out for viewing. I was too scared to really look at him. I only peeked at his corpse from behind my siblings. I wanted someone to comfort me, but no one did. It didn't make sense. Why was that memory back, as if I was reliving it? I was eight years old when that happened. Thoughts like those were disturbing, and vivid details made them feel more real than memories.

I needed a lot of pain medication just to cope with the pain. I was taking Darvocet, Valium and some other drugs. As if trauma, bad memories and sleep deprivation were not enough, I also had the side effects of my pain medications. All of this brought strange delusions and hallucinations. My hospital room was too warm for some of my visitors, but my body had a broken thermostat and to me it was wet and cold, and that shivering wouldn't go away. I was delirious at times. There were times when I was sure I had left the hospital.

One afternoon, a nurse was checking my blood pressure. I told her, "Sorry, I had to leave last night for a while. I went to visit my friend Delilah."

Once when my brother Pat was visiting me, I believed my room was filled with giant, clam-like monsters. When he came into the room, I warned him in a whisper, "Pat, these creatures… Don't look at them. They're going to kill you!"

Pat replied, "Katie, there's no one in this room but you and me."

I knew that was ridiculous; I could see the monsters! Our lives were in danger! I pleaded with Pat to listen to me.

I said, "I'm for real. You better leave. Don't you see those horrible creatures??? They're hovering around my damn bed, with blue and green seaweed floating around them!"

I could see by Pat's expression that he didn't believe me. He said, "Katie, calm down. We're fine."

I said, "Maybe you can't see them! It's a muddy mess in here."

Pat reached into his wallet and said, "Look, Katie, I'll bet you thirty dollars they won't kill me."

"No, they're coming for you. Get out of the way!" I was crying now.

Pat put his hand on my forehead and said, "Katie, you need to rest." His face looked sad and helpless.

"Okay," I replied -- and immediately saw the monsters eating my brother alive. It was violent, and very disgusting, and I couldn't do anything to stop it.

Aha, I thought to myself. *That was pretty bad - I tried to warn him about the monsters!*

Pat and I can laugh about all this now - but it wasn't funny to me then. I thought I was going crazy, except when I thought I was in mortal danger. It was either one or the other for many hours of the day.

I remember being convinced that I was living in a tree and that my bed was teetering on a limb too small to bear its weight; I saw lights flashing wildly; another time I was running and running, pursued by some wicked force. It was exhausting, it was gruesome, and I wouldn't wish it on anyone. It was by far the most frightened I've been in my life.

"I went to visit my friend Delilah again," I told the nurse.

"Katie, where are you? What date is it?" That brought me back to reality.

I used to beg my friends and family to stay with me overnight. I told them I needed their protection because certain people on the food service staff were taking me out of my hospital bed and performing witchcraft on me. Whoever was visiting me on those days would look sad – feeling sorry for me; perplexed because they could tell I believed what I was saying, and confused, because they didn't really know how to reply.

Those moments were pretty dark, and no one, including myself, was sure if I could or how I would recover.

Four Limbs Paralyzed

Whenever I looked at the wheelchair I thought "WTF"???

Two days after the spinal fusion surgery, I left the Intensive Care Unit for a regular hospital room. I was making progress!

Like most people, I had never spent much time thinking about my spinal cord before. Now, I learned all about it. The spinal cord is a sort of highway of information running from your brain to your rear end. The higher up the damage is on the spinal cord, the less you can feel and move.

A surgeon had been able to successfully wire my neck together. I was grateful for that.

On March 1, about three weeks after my accident, I had to get fitted for a "halo" to keep my neck immobile while it healed.

(Katie, March 1990)

There was nothing angelic about the halo. It was horrible and ugly, a plastic-and-metal body encasement, with two metal rods up the front, and two rods up the back. The rods are attached to a metal ring that goes around the skull above the eyebrow line and has bolts that are screwed into the skull itself, through the skin.

As they adjusted this and that, I felt like a side of beef on a rotisserie as I was fitted for my halo, and I hated the idea of having to wear it for three months. But there was nothing I could do about it; this was a crucial part of the road to my new life. I laid, they fitted.

I was paralyzed from the chest down… I was a quadriplegic, which is Greek for "four limbs paralyzed."

I cannot walk, I cannot move my legs or feet at all. I have no external feelings except on the inside of my arms and up through my thumbs. No sensation on the tops of my arms or in my curled paralyzed fingers. My fingers can be moved by others or even somewhat straightened, but a permanent curl gives me a great "scooping" ability.

I do have some "internal" sensations; stomach aches, a full bladder, and I sense poop moving down after a suppository has been administered. I do not sense direct feelings. When I experience a tingling sensation in my head and abdomen, I know something's going on and try to figure out what it is through deductive reasoning.

Remember, I was the girl who never sat still. Now, I was realizing there was going to be a whole lot of sitting. I did not get into the wheelchair until I could sit up without throwing up. Because of my inability to balance myself, I was dizzy whenever I tried. I had to overcome my challenges with balance in order to use the wheelchair without being sick. This took about a week for me to do – practicing in my bed – before they could wheel me to therapy without vomiting along the way.

My Body Is No Longer Mine Alone

There was also going to be a lot of time to think. The rest of my life was going to be spent having others take care of me and my body - because I wouldn't be able to care for myself.

I was pissed off. I was cold in my body, though I could barely feel it. I was hot in my mind, with the mounting anxiety about my present. I was frightened about the future. I was angry. Very angry. How could this have happened???

How could that car company sell an SUV that was unsafe, and prone to roll over? They must have known internally that it was unsafe… Wouldn't they know something like that?

Had God played any role in this happening to me? A nun from New York who visited me in Rehab certainly thought God had. She said, straight out, "Your accident; this is God's work. God did this."

After she'd left, I thought, *I don't think God's that mean. God didn't do it; God gets me through it.*

I realized I was going to miss the chance to do things on the spur of the moment, without planning. I had always been a spontaneous person but now, and for the rest of my life, it would be, *Do I have an attendant to go with me? Is the place we're going wheelchair-accessible? When will I have to empty my bladder?*

I also knew I was going to miss having feeling in my fingers, hands and in my body. I was going to miss wearing tall heels and doing my own hair. Strangely, I knew I would even miss cleaning house and cooking! Those days were difficult, to say the least. So much time to sit and think. I struggled to find the positives/possibilities in a seemingly impossible situation.

At the time I didn't realize it, but I had been more like my Dad than I ever thought. I had been busy working, busy moving, busy having fun. I was always on the go, and now, in this chair, I longed for more. I also knew that "before-the-accident Katie" would not have had the dedication, patience, and compassion to have been an aide to a quadriplegic. I hadn't had the disposition. Now that I had acquired the position to need an aide, I had to adopt the disposition to be a cooperative quadriplegic.

Much of what I longed for was not to be possible, yet I found value in deep conversations. I now had time. I wanted people to sit down with me and really talk. Being in a wheelchair does that for you.

I needed to have patience and my accident had forced me to slow down enough to learn to care.

I Became Grateful for My Family's Support

My family sacrificed a lot to pull me through.

My Recovery Was a Family Effort

After the accident, my family was very good to me. Yes, we have a deeply rooted hierarchy and yes, we have natures which are often more competitive than cooperative. But we Rodríguez's also have a deep desire to help and, in a crisis, my family can become "a SWAT team of love."

The day after the accident, my mother wanted to see me. As she aged Mom was overweight with limited energy and low blood sugar, and she also experienced anxiousness and palpitations. The doctors said no, she should wait until my recovery was farther along. They said it would be too upsetting. They were concerned for her and she didn't need to see me just then.

They didn't know my mother. She may have looked and seemed like a pushover, but when it came to her children, she would find the strength, energy and courage. When the doctors and nurses saw she meant business, they let her in.

When she first saw me, broken and so drugged up, she broke down wailing and crying. She grieved for me and wondered what type of life I would have in my state. But Mom quickly realized that grief and sadness were not going to help her nor me with my new living situation. After the initial shock of seeing my current condition, Mom bounced right back and was determined to help me recover.

My mother established a new routine while I was in the hospital. She sat by my bedside and read to me. She fed me ice chips when my mouth was so dry because I couldn't swallow easily. She removed the dry masses from my tongue and the side of my mouth. I felt like I was two years old again, and maybe Mom did, too.

They had me strapped in place on a bed that tilted slowly, from one side to the other. In the 30 years since then, a whole new generation of hospital beds has come along, air-cushioned, run by electricity and are much more comfortable. But in 1990, when they turned me in bed, to prevent bedsores, I yelled, "Mom, no! This hurts too much! Stop this! Mom, this sucks!"

She replied, "Now, Katie, this is for your own good. So, you hang in there, my little chickie."

She'd bring me in a cute new top to wear, or some lipstick. She always seemed to be at my side, keeping my mind occupied, showing me, I wouldn't have to go through this alone.

Over and over again, she sang, "You Are My Sunshine." There I was griping and swearing, and she was singing that I was her sunshine, the girl who kept her happy when skies were gray.

One day, Mom brought in my cassette player with some of my favorite tapes. There was some classical music, and rock' n' roll songs by the Cars. I closed my eyes and lost myself in the music, *"It Was Just What I Needed."*

The first time I moved my right arm, you would have thought Mom had won the lottery. People would come to visit, and Mom, my greatest cheerleader would say, "C'mon, Katie, show them what you can do!"

It made me feel a little like a sea lion at the zoo - but it taught me to celebrate *any* accomplishment. Mom, being my nearly constant companion when I was in the hospital, was like an angel to me.

***

My family, unbeknownst to me at the time, was already planning for my journey beyond the walls. They knew I would need support and constant care. My older sister Eileen, her husband Bill, and their 2-year-old daughter, Maddie, moved from Kansas City to St. Louis, just so Eileen could help me out. Packing up their whole lives just to take care of me, yeah, grateful is an understatement!

Genuine Friendship

Especially after the accident, I felt what friendship and love were all about, and learned to appreciate them.

Getting paralyzed will show you who your real friends are. Some people I thought cared about me dropped me as soon as they realized I was never getting out of this wheelchair. After the accident, some people just didn't want to look at me. I realize that some felt having a disability was shameful, or a disease they could catch. Some couldn't or didn't want to imagine themselves in my condition, so it was easier to look away.

But other people stepped forward - like Kelly, a friend from Kirkwood High, who came to visit me in the hospital several times, and brought her young daughter, Amanda. I loved their visits.

Delilah, My Friend

Delilah, who was the driver, had walked away from the accident with a few ugly bumps and bruises. Her face had been scarred a little from the windshield glass – but everything healed, and she was okay. She came to visit me in the hospital quite a few times.

Sharon, who hadn't been wearing a seat belt, was launched through the canvas roof of the car during the rollover, had contusions and both her ears were detached. But she was able to walk away from the accident, too.

And I, who *had* been wearing a seat belt, got a broken neck, an injured spinal cord, a fractured jaw, fractured hip, fractured ribs, crushed shoulder blade, punctured lung and a damaged kidney.

Life isn't fair.

I knew it was hard for Delilah to visit, to see me paralyzed, but she kept coming.

Once, during one of Delilah's visits, I asked her, "Hey, why doesn't Sharon visit me?"

Delilah replied sadly, "Sharon just can't handle seeing you like this."

I sighed and said, "That's a bummer." But I knew Sharon was young and active, the type of person who didn't have much time and patience for simply sitting or hanging out. She wanted to be doing something all the time. Come to think of it, we probably had more in common "pre-accident" than I would like to admit.

Delilah sat silently and, with a sad look in her eyes, murmured, "I'm sorry."

I countered, "Don't worry, Sharon is no big loss."

"No, Katie, I'm sorry about *all this*," and she pointed to my body, and all the equipment around the room that was needed because of my disability.

In the sweetest voice I could summon, I said, "I know you are."

"Katie, I feel just awful," Delilah said with care.

I said, "Look, Delilah, this happened, and nothing can change that."

She said, "How can you feel that way? I mean, if it were the other way around..." She trailed off.

I said, "Look, what is... is. I just appreciate you being here, visiting, and being my friend. Staying close, that's what you can do."

I wasn't being noble; I was being rational. The deep guilt Delilah felt was an awful burden for her, and one that couldn't do either of us any good.

"Don't carry that burden -- at least not for my sake. Visit me," I shared.

That conversation was powerful for the both of us because it was truly a lesson of acknowledgement, acceptance and letting go. I was still a very young woman, but learning forgiveness was one of the things that freed my mind and soul, allowing me to heal.

Woody

My college friend, Woody, came to see me often. When I had my surgery, Woody was there, alongside my Mom. They bit their nails off together. One fine day, she brought our friend Pam, who put cold cream on my dry face, and that felt wonderful. As you can tell, I was growing to appreciate the little things that made all the difference.

(The Four Amigas, four months before paralysis, 1989)

Woody had a phobia about hospitals, but she came anyway. When she saw the Darvocet and the Valium and the other heavy narcotics, and she said, "Katie, you are on some heavy drugs." I was, and one of those drugs gave me nightmares about dying. Through her own fears, she was great to me, and let me talk about my dreams of dying, even though they scared her. She cried right in front of me, even though she didn't want to. She was a true friend.

Woody also reminded me I was getting a lot of mail from people who had heard about the accident. A volleyball team I had recently joined sent a postcard. I appreciated her keeping me in touch/connected with people and happenings outside of my hospital room.

On the serious side of things, Woody kept a journal of that time, written in the form of a personal letter to me. Later, she gave that journal to me, which was very thoughtful of her. It made me feel like I hadn't missed much in my current state. This documentation was a validation of my ability to deal with the circumstance at hand.

She made a great point when she reminded me that she didn't love me because of my body, but because I cared about her, and had taken the time to get to know her -- and none of that would have to change.

Woody also usually had a joke to tell me when she came, and so would my family members.

One day, Woody arrived just after I'd been given a dose of the "good stuff." I was singing out, at the top of my lungs, "Sh*t, sh*t, sh*t!"

Mom was sitting there with me, doing her needlepoint. She whispered to Woody, without missing a beat, "Katie's having a bad day."

After a terrible accident, many visitors say something like, "I'm sorry this happened to you." But, if I can make a suggestion here, it's much better to keep track of the progress of the accident victim and say, "I'm proud of you." That's what Woody did.

Not too long into my hospital stay, Woody told me that she and her boyfriend, Richard, were considering getting married, on the 10th anniversary of their first date. She warned me I better be ready to be her maid of honor. The thought of that was thrilling and scary at the same time! Knowing the wedding was coming, it gave me hope and incentive to "get prepared" and further reason to work hard to be part of the wedding party.

***

Roseanne, My New Friend

As I've mentioned, creativity and music flow to and through me, naturally. I soon realized music was going to help save me. A few weeks after I got out of Intensive Care downtown, an ambulance took me to St. John's Mercy Medical Center, a hubbub of activity in St. Louis County. After my two months of Intensive Care, I was lucky to get four more months of Rehabilitation. I felt well cared for there.

My roommate Roseanne was tall, had blonde hair, was in her 60s and had Multiple Sclerosis. I loved her right away. She was maternal without being overbearing, which I found comforting during that hard time.

As she said, "I'm walking one day and paralyzed the next. It comes and goes, and I wish it would leave me the hell alone!"

When the lights went out that first night, I became very depressed and scared with this change in residency. I was crying uncontrollably. Roseanne heard me and saw the tears rolling down my cheeks. Though she was very weak, she crawled out of her bed and stood next to me.

I said, "You aren't supposed to get out of your bed."

She replied, "I don't care."

She put her arms around me, and said, "What can I do?"

I said, "I'm really scared, and I can't sleep." I whispered, "Rosanne, do you know the words to *Amazing Grace*?"

She said, "One of God's Top Ten!"

We started singing together:

> *"Amazing Grace, how sweet the sound*
>
> *That saved a wretch like me*
>
> *I once was lost but now am found*
>
> *Was blind but now I see..."*

We sang "Amazing Grace" through the night. We sang that song until we were too tired to carry the tune and, thankfully, until my fear subsided.

After that night, I often sang when I felt scared or unsure.

During my six months of hospitalization, I dealt with the pain and stress in my own way: I became known as the "Singing Patient." The technicians enjoyed drawing my blood because they knew they would get a free concert.

***

In the Light of Friendship

Little did I know that 20 months after getting out of Rehab, in October of 1991, when Woody and Richard got married, I did make it to Woody's wedding. I felt honored to serve as Woody's Maid of Honor. She, and the entire wedding party embraced me and my wheelchair.

It was a simple church of crosses and pews. One groomsman had rolled out some beautiful paper on the aisle, and another one of them pushed me in a manual wheelchair whose tires horribly wrinkled the paper. Woody followed me down the aisle with a big smile on her face. Though it was a truly beautiful occasion, I struggled. As prepared as I tried to be, I didn't feel fully included in the wedding party – but that was my fault, not hers, after all, I was just getting adjusted to being On A Roll, especially in public, and in front of strangers.

> *There is little comfort when fighting for one's life – so my friends were literally my lifeline at times. Finding joy, especially through pain takes time and effort, and my friends are a Godsend.*

PART THREE

Learning to Roll

Hanging on to hope, you learn to cope with what you are given. When you soar, obtaining more, then you are truly living.

Dealing with the fatigue that comes with the ever-present pain in life takes daily effort. I have developed coping mechanisms that have enabled me to deal with what comes my way. I share them with the hope to help people overcome personal challenges, from which no one is immune.

Katie's Coping Strategies

Feel It   Reveal what you feel. You make it real.

Think It   Start to reflect. You'll gain respect.

Write It   Use paper and pen, revealing again.

Say It   Saying it out loud will make you feel proud.

I practice using all four of my coping mechanisms regularly, but I have found that writing has helped me the most. When I write, I sit patiently, waiting for the words to come. Sometimes I can journal for hours, at other times, a poem pops right out of my brain and onto the paper. I like it when the words just flow, but that doesn't always happen, so in between those great moments I write what I can.

Sometimes this process takes minutes. Other times, mastering change takes hours, days, weeks, or more. Change stops for no one. Change is inevitable, so it's important to adapt.

Learning to Function and Flourish

People go by and they look at me.
I wonder when they look, what do they see?
Perhaps a person who hasn't a life
who just sits in a chair with a life that's not right.
But if they looked deeper, it's not all what it seems.
I am a woman. I have feelings. I have hope. I have dreams.

(Katie Applying Makeup, 1992)

My experience in Rehab taught me how to live in my current body – and it was life-changing, eye-opening and even heart-warming as my caretakers rallied around me.

Rehabilitation

ehab is about learning to take baby steps, one after the other. How to sit up in bed a little without vomiting. How to feed yourself with an eating splint attached to your hand. How to brush your teeth with a brace and brush-head that wraps around your hand. Building up your skills and building up your stamina. And it really is a slow process.

A low point for me was the day a Rehab nurse was showing Woody how to catheterize, or cath me. What this means is my bottoms are pulled to my ankles, my feet are placed heel to heel, and a cath kit is opened. A cath kit contains sterile rubber gloves, a pack of betadine swabs, a tube and a receptacle. Sometimes the receptacle is a plastic container and sometimes it is a plastic bag with the tube inside of it. My half-naked body is spread-eagled, leaving me with the feelings of humiliation and embarrassment. It really hit home that day, that for the rest of my life, I could only have privacy for as long as I could hold my bladder. I'd need help with bathing, meal preparation, household help, my personal finances - with everything.

With those thoughts in my mind, cathing suddenly seemed callous and sterile to me, and everything smelled and tasted like metal. Cathing was hard, cold and impersonal; I was going to have to submit to it for the rest of my life, and I couldn't do anything about it but lie there and cry.

My crying disturbed the nurse and Woody and they tried to comfort me. Finally, I told myself, *Katie, it's either this or you lie in a hospital bed with no life at all, attached to a catheter.*

I had to deal with "phantom pain" -- a jarring tingling in parts of my body that, formally speaking, do not feel pain. This is quite common; I've met a lot of amputees who feel tingling in fingers or toes that are no longer there. But knowing this is common or "well-known in the medical literature" doesn't really help. The tingling is unpleasant, and I've never really gotten used to it.

I slept with my fingers wrapped around a cone that made my fingers remain curled. I am happy they did this because now I can flex and extend my wrist to pick up small objects like raisins, fruits, nuts, and important foods like M&Ms.

Karen, My Psychotherapist

Once I was hospitalized and stable, Karen and I continued our sessions with her coming to see me. Always so composed, I could tell upon her first vision of me in that bed, she was shocked, though she tried to keep it from me.

"Now, Katie," she whispered to me, "Life, as you have known it, is on hold. This will be one of the biggest challenges ever set before you - but I do know you are capable of dealing with this."

She got me to do hypnotic meditations. She called it "visioning" and she made me see that I could learn to slip out of my horribly damaged body and examine myself from a distance.

I've always had a good and vivid imagination. Before long, I was able to close my eyes, listen to Karen's mellow voice, and be back in the woods across the street from my childhood house. In my mind, I was hiking and smelling the flowers. I could almost feel myself running down the giant hill again, my legs pumping, my heart pounding, feeling a breeze rush by me...

Visioning felt so much better than the hospital bed. It also prepared me for what was in store...

Beth, My PT

Beth was my physical therapist ("PT"). I called her my "Physical Terrorist." Beth was lean and strong. She had a quiet smile, and with her muscles, she moved me like I weighed one pound.

Actually, Beth reminded me of my old self, the aerobics instructor who used to call out, "Come on, Ladies! Move it or lose it!" That used to make the ladies laugh. I thought, *I've got to have a better sense of humor. If three quarters of my body's going to be immobile, I'm going to move the other quarter all I can.*

I had someone bring in some of my favorite '80s music: Michael Jackson, "*Wanna Be Startin' Somethin*" and the Talking Heads, "*And She Was.*" I told Beth, "If you're going to torture me, torture me *to a beat.*" The music made Beth's torture bearable.

Beth helped me to like my body again.

Lori, My OT

Lori was my occupational therapist ("OT") with bouncy, curly hair, she was a high-energy girlie girl with a very pretty smile. She was a skilled therapist with gleaming eyes and great professional skill. She helped build my confidence while I was learning.

About four months after my accident, Lori fitted me for a "tenodesis brace," or what I call my bionic hand. She wanted me to master using the assistive technology that was available to me. My brace has three Velcro straps that wrap around my forearm and hand and metal pieces that wrap around my thumb and first two fingers. The brace opens and closes the fingers and thumb on my right hand. She patiently showed me how to use a writing brace which would also allow me to type on a keyboard, and a 3-strap brace, so I could bring a fork or spoon to my mouth and feed myself. We also put a hook on the back of my electric toothbrush. I was doing pretty good, learning things.

Lori was sensitive and caring, but she also wanted me to see where I was, and where I could go. She encouraged me to look in a mirror and see myself. When she held that mirror in front of my face, I cried. God, did I cry - because I didn't feel pretty anymore.

I had won the Kirkwood Junior Miss competition. I had once won a wet t-shirt contest at a bar, despite competing against someone who dropped her underwear! And now I didn't feel like a woman at all; I felt like an "it."

I couldn't believe that reflection in the mirror was actually me. How could I show my face or contribute anything to society looking like this? How could I be happy?

At that moment I realized I would have to fight to regain my womanhood…

Lori started to show me how I could regain my femininity. Early in my recovery, I told Lori, "I'm not leaving Rehab until I can put on my own lipstick!"

She told me I was the first one of her patients to ever want to put on makeup, and she was happy to show me how to do it. She even made me a brace that held the wand for my mascara.

Lori put rubber tubing around my make-up brushes and eye liner so that I could learn to apply them myself. It took me a few tries. After I had gotten the hang of it, I was so excited! I enjoyed lining my eyes, coloring my cheeks, and applying my favorite lipstick. When I was done, I wheeled around my fellow patients, showing off my accomplishment. God, it was good to feel pretty again!

A few days later, Lori asked if she could videotape me using my new-found beauty talent and routine to inspire others who may feel discouraged. I was delighted at the request. Of course, I agreed! Since this was back in the days before social media, she set up a camcorder along with a radio playing classical music in the background.

I started the video with, "Okay ladies, you have to make the most of what you have, and just a little dab will do you!"

The video lasted about five minutes. And afterward, I felt fulfilled in a way I hadn't in quite a while. Being able to physically enhance my beauty while encouraging others to do the same was uplifting and important. And then I looked up and saw tears in Lori's eyes. She was proud of me and so full of emotions. She made a profound difference in my life, and I made a difference in hers. The hospital shared the video with newly injured women, after their arrival in Rehab. Little did I know at the time, this would be a foretelling of what life would hold for me, living *On A Roll*.

***

Finding Beauty in Simplicity

Now, I keep my haircut simple and sassy, easy for my personal care attendants to style. It's a treat to find an aide who's good with a hair dryer and a curling iron. It is hard to though, to find clothes that look cute on a permanently seated person. Just a tweak here and there can make all the difference, and I'm always on the lookout for new ways to make the bad look good. I'm also addicted to secondhand clothing stores. I can buy more for less and it's always new to me.

***

Everyone Responds to Rehab Differently

When I was able to *embrace* Rehab, I reached a turning point. I fully surrendered and took on the responsibility to improve my body and, with that, my mind. Instead of thinking of Rehab as something to be endured, I began to see that it was expanding my horizons, opening doors for me. If I embraced it and pushed harder, more doors would open.

I decided to deal with what was happening to me, physically, emotionally and mentally as well. In the meantime, I had to work on being happier. In fact, one grumpy male quadriplegic and the other, a grumpy paraplegic in Rehab repeatedly asked me, "Katie, why are you always so damn happy?"

I'd give them a big smile and answer, "I don't know." Then I'd roll on to whatever the therapists told me was next.

I do know something about this – about choosing to be happy. I believe that happiness is a choice, something we must consciously select. During my darkest, scariest moments, I began thinking about things I love, things that bring me joy and happiness, and to focus on those things. I continued to sing, hum, and listen to good music.

When I was being cathed, I thought about things outside of the hospital that I enjoyed eating, visiting or experiencing. I smiled when I thought about the diversity of St. Louis, the people, the languages, and the places. My taste buds tingled when I thought of the way toasted ravioli is made in St. Louis. And I envisioned seeing the architecture of the old Courthouse Building, Bevo Mill, the Arch, as well as the city skyline at night. I couldn't wait to get outside and enjoy the lovely warm summer days, appreciating more than ever, the beautiful sunsets. I determined to be happy, and was determined to once again, experience life beyond those hospital walls, with my wheelchair being my new, constant companion.

Of course, it was difficult to smile some days. It was difficult to feel happy, but as long as I consciously selected it, I knew I would thrive. I saw some people in Rehab who just gave up. One guy left Rehab unable to even feed himself. His Mom and I had become acquainted and she asked me, "Max should learn how to feed himself, shouldn't he?"

I nodded 'Yes.'

He could have learned to, but he chose not to. I doubt he's still alive. Being paralyzed was tough. And, I was learning that the tougher the hand we've been dealt by life, the more we have to make a priority to choose happiness – through it all – and forgiving others, is a continuous process.

Another guy told me, "I was an asshole before my disability - and I'm not changing!" I thought, *Good luck trying to get someone to wipe your butt.*

Then there was the woman in her 50's who was recovering from a stroke. At least she was supposed to be recovering. But being negative and complaining was what she was really doing. She moaned and groaned all the time. She refused to try.

One night, again and again, she called out, "My back, my back, help me! My back, my back, help me!"

Finally, I was so fed up with her disturbances that I shouted down the hall, "Look, Lady, all of us are in pain in one way or another. Put a lid on it!"

She did - sort of. The next morning, when I rolled down to Rehab, I got a round of applause from some of my neighbors in the hall.

Going Out, in Public

My chair is an automatic head turner and something I can't hide, so I had to get comfortable being my own parade.

My first venture out of the Rehab hospital was going out for pizza with a few other "wheelers." Still encased in my halo, strapped to a manual wheelchair, I rolled into the hospital van scared as hell.

Judy, the Recreation therapist, loaded me and my chair into the van. My mother was there, too. Mom and Judy were glad I'd agreed to go out in public. They thought this was a great idea.

But when our caravan of wheelchairs rolled into the pizza parlor, I felt so self-conscious. We were quite the motley crew: stroke survivors, paraplegics, quadriplegics…

I swear every patron in the restaurant seemed to be staring at us. Some of their cold glares made me want to crawl into a hole and never come out. I felt like a member of a freak show, and I wanted to leave. But we stayed in the pizza parlor.

After the pizza parlor, my next outing was to a movie theater to see Julia Roberts in "Pretty Woman." While waiting my turn to get out of the van, I looked out the window and saw two girls standing next to their bikes, holding tennis rackets in one hand and ice cream cones in the other, licking their ice cream cones and talking happily to each other.

I felt a stab of pain because those two girls reminded me so much of an old friend, Julia, and me, the way we used to ride bikes and play tennis… Now I could never do either of those things again. I cried the whole way back to Rehab.

My Mother-Aide in Training

Caring for my new needs was a learning experience for all. The pizza outing had gone okay, so I agreed to come home to a family party in July at Mom and Dad's house.

I'd been sad when my parents had sold our house on Joe Avenue, the home I grew up in. However, it turned out that the house my parents had moved to in Glendale was much better for my needs as a wheeler. Their willingness to support my new reality really knew no boundaries.

Mom was trained to catheterize me. She had watched a nurse do it, then, under the nurse's supervision, so she was confident she could do it by herself.

My first sterile cath kits were hospital grade. The kits included: a small, rectangular plastic bucket; a long, skinny rubber tube; a small cotton wipe; three betadine cotton swabs; and a pair of latex gloves. With each piece came the risk of exposure to more bacteria. All of the separate parts, I know contributed to the number of bladder infections I developed. Once I discovered the cath kits I use now, with a sterile tube attached to a bag, my bladder infections became easier to keep at bay.

The hospital let me leave Rehab for the party. At my request, I asked my nurse to decorate my "halo" with daisies and ribbons.

(Katie, May 1990)

My brother Tom got me and my halo into the back seat of my Dad's Ford Escort, drove me to Mom and Dad's and got me out of the car. He put me in a light-weight manual wheelchair and served as my driver.

When we reached the front door, someone yelled, "Katie's here!"

Right then, I knew it was going to be a loud, wild Rodriguez get together and I was glad to be part of it. The aroma of barbecue cooking on a grill. Laughter drifting through open windows. Seeing all my mother's antiques again. Little kids running around in a pack. I was so happy.

An hour into the party, I had that vague feeling that told me I needed to pee, and things began to fall apart. I called out, "Yo, Tom! I need a cath."

Tom and Pat gently lifted me out of my wheelchair and placed me on my parents' bed – but, without the nurse there to guide her, Mom couldn't figure out how to cath me. I tried to explain but I couldn't get her to see what I was talking about. Mom tried and tried but could get no pee in the skinny rubber tube. Eileen came in and tried to help, but she hadn't been trained in how to cath someone.

So, then I had to be dressed again, put back in my wheelchair, and then transferred to the back seat with my wheelchair loaded into the trunk of the Ford Escort. Tom drove me back to the hospital – all so I could pee. I was totally frustrated, and sad. I realized that the rest of my life could be like this. I felt like a tire losing all its air. I didn't return to the party that day, after I was cathed. I did decide that if I had anything to do with it, I would not have one of those experiences again – I deserved to pee properly and continue to party!

Mom confessed to me that she felt guilty that she hadn't been able to cath me. I consoled her. I wanted to boost her confidence for the long road ahead of us. We were in this for the long haul and needed each other. Shortly after the family party, mom came back to the hospital, and watched again, very carefully, as the nurses showed her where to insert the tube.

"Oh!" said Mom. "It's *that* hole!"

Come to find out, she'd been sticking the tube into my clitoris instead of my urethra! (Thank God I couldn't feel it.)

Yes, I'm proud of being a woman -- but sometimes I wish I had a penis. Cathing would be a whole lot easier!

Rehab with Dad

Rehabilitation prepared me to live as a person with a disability. Since I had always loved taking care of my body, the direction I was given eased some of the burdens I was now facing. Exercising replaced moments of sadness I sometimes experienced post injury.

Dealing with Rehab, I was greatly helped by Karen, my psychotherapist, the nurses and my Dad. Being stuck in a manual wheelchair, and re-learning to function gave my dad and me the time and space to have an actual connection. My father's presence during my most difficult time revealed his vulnerable, sensitive side, that place in him I had always longed to experience.

After three months, I was stronger, and my neck had healed enough to get my "halo" taken off. My father went with me on the ambulance ride from St. John's back to Barnes Hospital for the procedure.

At Barnes Hospital, I was propped up on a table, stabilized by my father and two nurses. The doctor made sure that the three of them had a good hold on me, and then loosened the two screws in my forehead and the two in the back of my head. Since my neck muscles had atrophied, when the four metal rods no longer held up my head, my head dropped like a bowling ball.

I could not lift my head at all. That was one of my worst moments. I was humiliated. I felt reduced to something pitiful and, for a while, I wanted to die.

The nurses took the stern, tough approach with me. "Hold your head up, Katie!" They wouldn't take no for an answer.

Incredibly, it was Dad, who had yelled at me so often when I was a girl, who took the gentle approach now. He looked at me with heartache in his eyes. With love. He was now 69 years old, and he'd mellowed with age, with asthma and by surviving three heart attacks.

He said, "Katie, you can do this! We'll put a foam brace around your neck... You'll keep going... C'mon, you can do this!"

Through my tears, I looked into his eyes and I believed him. There in the hospital, for the first time in my life, Dad really saw my sadness. He looked like a different man. For the first time in my life, I felt a true and loving connection with my father. In those moments, all was right in my world.

Bathing

Before my accident, my pain tolerance was always low, and it still is. Paper cuts, bee stings, splinters in my feet, medical shots in the doctor's office, I'd cry. I hated being cold or hungry. But suddenly, since the accident, I no longer felt much of my body. Splinters and paper cuts were not an issue. Now that the halo was off, my dad and I had connected, and I was worn out from the ambulance ride back to Rehab, *That's it*, I thought, when I got back to my hospital bed. *No more challenges. I need rest.*

But the nurses knew I needed constant challenges, to build myself up so that one day I could go back out into the world again. Soon one of my favorite nurses came into the room and said, "Now that your halo is off, guess what you get to have?"

"What?" I asked, very sarcastically.

She smiled and said, "A bath - and we can even throw some bubbles in it."

I was instantly excited! Three months of bed baths was enough.

I was bathed, dried and clean clothes were put on me. I quickly got over my sarcastic attitude and went back to my Rehab with a vengeance.

Soon, I was able to eat, to write my own name, and put on my own make-up.

Dad would come into my room, see me all dolled up, smile and say, "Just beautiful, Katie!"

As I got to thinking about everything that had happened, I decided it was not so bad. Yes, I had lost something physically, no question about it. But my physical looks were going to fade with age anyway. The best things about me were my smarts, my sass, and my deep desire to make the world a better, freer, and a fairer place. After the accident, all of that idealism was still there in me. I had gained so much, and had much to do, but first I had to get out of Rehab.

Dad and the Chair

I learned how to drive my wheelchair a lot faster than I learned to drive a car. In Rehab I realized that I didn't have the strength to push a manual wheelchair. So, after I was discharged from the hospital, a power wheelchair was delivered to my parents' house and I couldn't wait to drive it.

But my Dad said, "No, let's take it to the hospital and they'll train you on how to use it!"

I knew I could drive the chair without hospital training, but my Dad insisted that I have proper training. He took me, my manual wheelchair and the power wheelchair to the hospital. My therapist transferred me to the new wheelchair and put five miniature orange cones on the floor, as a course for me to navigate.

"Now, you be careful, young lady!" said my Dad.

I hit the green "Go" button and sailed through the course, never even grazing one of those orange cones. I drove and drove, zooming around the room. I felt so free!

Dad looked so proud of me that I laughed out loud.

Finding Beauty in the Bad

One afternoon, my sister took me out for a ride in her car and decided to pull into a drug store and pick up a prescription. I said, "You run in and get what you need," and she hopped out. I was learning the art of waiting when a car pulled up by my open window.

A grumpy older man emerged from a car with a cane and moaned as he moved. I said, "Hello, how are you?"

"I've been better," he snarled.

"Me, too."

"My legs are stiff, and walking isn't easy."

"Yes," I said "and I'm sorry, but at least you can walk."

"Yes, young lady, you are right. Thanks for the reminder."

I said, "Well, you're catching me on a good day!"

Accepting physical limitations is hard, and accepting mental limitations is harder. Anxiety and depression are rampant in society. I could tell that my cheerful reminder brightened that man's day. At least I gave him a different perspective on the abilities he'd lost and those he still had.

Feelings help dictate our actions and attitudes. Feeling feminine, again, helped my healing, especially emotionally and mentally.

With all of the skilled professionals teaching me vital skills, surrounded by patient loved ones, I felt super self-empowered and ready for whatever came next.

Moving Back Home

I was hesitant about living with my parents again...

When I got out of Rehabilitation, I moved back into my parents' home. I knew living with Mom would be fine, but Dad… I was encouraged but unsure how things would go.

Because of my disability, I was going to be spending a lot of time in the house. I wondered if things would be the same as they'd been when I was a girl and Dad was the dictator of the house. It turned out they were quite different.

In the past, I think Dad had felt uncomfortable with my youthful energy and antics as a young woman. As a matter of fact, just shortly before the accident, dad had caught me in bed with a guy. And to make matters worse, it was in his bed, the one he shared with mom. After chasing the dude out of the house, my dad continued to be livid. For three weeks, he wouldn't even look at me. Though I was still youthful, there was little chance I was going to be having sex in my parents' bed, this go round. Yet, being who we both were, pre-accident, we ran the risk of butting heads and hurting each other's feelings. We treaded lightly…

My disability put my life in slow motion. I started searching for resources to assist me.

Early on, my sister Eileen and my sister-in-law Carroll often served as my afternoon attendants. They both learned how to cath me and transfer me in and out of their vehicles. Pre-cell phones and laptops, every other week, Carroll and I went on trips throughout the St. Louis area to investigate who was doing what in serving the needs of people with disabilities.

One day we were in front of the Missouri Division of Vocational Rehabilitation office. Carroll was transferring me from the front seat of her car to my manual wheelchair, when it started rolling away. We'd forgotten to secure the locks on my chair. Instead of panicking, we both started cracking up. Carroll had my legs between her legs, my arms were wrapped around her shoulders and she was about ready to drop me when a young man came by and helped us. He grabbed my chair and held it still as Carroll put me in it. Woo hoo, I was saved to roll another day!

My First Job Post Rehab

A few months after my discharge, I did some volunteer work for St. John's Mercy Medical Center, calling former patients to find out how well or poorly they were doing. I sat in front of a desk in my parents' second bedroom, using a speaker phone. "Hi! I'm here to follow up…"

Some of these former patients had improved a lot; others had not. Some were pleased to take the call; others were not. A few times, a spouse or relative answered the phone and informed me the patient had died.

I got to talk to some people whom I had known in Rehab. I can't write well in small spaces, so I had to have the forms enlarged for me. After a few months, there was no one left to call, I'd gotten through all. Connecting with everyone had given me a lot of satisfaction. Though I was volunteering, I took my job seriously. It gave me purpose.

Working from home and enjoying meals and time with my parents gave us time to ease into a new rhythm. The anxiety of the unknown had caused me stress. I was still in my mind, wondering how my father and I would deal with one another.

Dad had been gentle and encouraging in the hospital, yes. But he still hadn't spoken to me in any depth about his life and mine. We hadn't been able to have real conversations in the hospital.

Now, we did. Dad would push my wheelchair out on the patio, and we'd talk. We had some great conversations! I learned many things about Dad which I'd never known, and there was peace between us as never before. Time, asthma attacks, and grandkids had all played a part in mellowing Dad.

Dad's old threat, "Quit crying or I'll give you something to cry about!" seemed like something out of another lifetime. I cried sometimes and Dad accepted this. Both of us had learned that crying isn't so bad. In fact, in small doses it can be pretty darn good, and a great stress reliever. Shoving that emotion down deep inside, refusing to deal with it… that's what's bad.

I think God knew I'd live a fuller life if I could learn to slow down enough to listen, laugh, and love. And I believe God helped my father to see the vulnerable woman beneath my exterior.

Living with my parents, this time around was more than I could have ever imagined, and I was better because of the loving- closeness with my Dad.

Left on The Dance Floor

A painful reality, and something I had no control over is how I can try to describe what happened with my old boyfriend, Jeff.

One of the many people who had visited me in the hospital was my old high school boyfriend Jeff. Back in the day, we had been quite the active couple.

While I was in Rehab, he brought a rose in a vase, and put it on the nightstand next to my hospital bed. "Hey, girl," he said.

"Hey, boy," I said right back at him.

He looked deeply into my eyes. "How are you?"

"Well, I've been better."

"Yes, I'm sure." Then he leaned over my bed, put his face between the metal bars of my halo, and kissed me. His lips were so warm, and it felt just like before. I was in heaven.

That kiss made clear to me that at least my hormones hadn't been paralyzed. They'd just been sleeping, and now Jeff had awakened them. I felt great for hours after.

My body was so altered, I had such severe doubts that I was going to be the theatrical beauty I'd once been. In a way, I was a virgin all over again.

Before Jeff left, he said to me: "Hey, once you get out of here, let's hook up. Cool?"

"Sure," I said. Now *there* was some real incentive to survive what had happened to me!

Now living with my parents, Woody wanted to help me build up a social life again. She called me at my parents' home and said, "Hey, Katie, how would you like to go out on the town Friday night and then spend the night over here? I figure your folks would rather you do that than have to put your butt to bed at one in the morning!"

I laughed and replied: "Cool. Can I invite someone to meet us at Calico's for a drink?"

"Sounds good to me," said Woody.

I called Jeff and asked if he wanted to meet me and my friends for a drink. He said he did. My head was in the clouds! Maybe I had a real boyfriend again! Or maybe not. Wondering about Jeff's intentions was making me a nervous wreck.

My Mom helped me to get ready for my date with Jeff. Then came a knock on my parents' front door -- Woody and Richard, her later to-be husband. Richard rolled me out the door and down the gray wooden ramp that my brother Pat had built for my wheels.

Richard and Woody loaded me and my wheelchair into their car, and we took off. Woody asked with a giggle, "Is your prince meeting us at Calico's?"

"Yes!" I squealed.

Even if I couldn't jump up and down, I felt as if I could.

"Chhhhoool!" said Richard, in his best "Beavis and Butthead" voice.

We got to Calico's and Jeff was waiting out front. We found a table for four and ordered drinks. It smelled like a bar, and laughter and warm bodies were all around us. I could only have one Pina colada because alcohol didn't mix with my medications, but that was a bit of creamy coconut yumminess. Calico's was a little noisy, but we had a nice four-way talk.

After a while, the noise from the bar got so loud we couldn't carry on a decent conversation anymore. Jeff seemed a little stiff. Richard yelled, "Hey, let's go over to our place and hang out!"

This was a big moment for me. If Jeff was repulsed by seeing me in a wheelchair, this was the time for him to say 'You know, it's getting late. I'm going to take off now, but it's been great seeing you, Katie,' shake hands with Richard and Woody, give me a quick peck on the cheek, and walk away.

But Jeff didn't do that. He said "Sure." He had a heart, and my heart leaped. I noticed what a pleasantly warm St. Louis evening it was.

Richard pushed my wheelchair toward his parked car.

Jeff said, "Do you want to come in my car?"

"Sure," I said with a huge smile.

But as Richard and Woody loaded me and my chair into Jeff's two-door hatchback, Jeff had a look of uncertainty. He didn't look excited to be with me, and that was deflating.

I took a deep breath: "Would you buckle my seatbelt for me?"

"Okay," he said, and I heard the belt click in place.

Things were fine at first but when Jeff made a sharp left turn, the seatbelt couldn't hold me in place, and I fell toward Jeff. Just because I was aware of all the different parts of my body didn't mean I could use them.

"Oh, God, I'm sorry. I didn't mean to," he said. He looked anxious as he pushed me back up straight.

I tried to ease his mind by laughing and saying, "I don't do sharp turns very well." When he still looked anxious, I added, "I'm a wobbly passenger. Don't worry about it. I've been through a lot worse!" I laughed again, but Jeff was silent.

Woody and Richard brought me and Jeff into their apartment, got me set up on the couch and then left us alone.

This time it was Jeff who was paralyzed. I said, "Sit down. I don't bite too hard." I laughed again, but he looked at me with pity and despair. After what seemed like an eternity, Jeff said, "I should go" and bolted out the door.

A few months later, I received a letter from him which said,

> Katie,
>
> *I cannot explain my quick departure weeks back. I have totally taken my body for granted all my life. You are so accepting of your situation.*
>
> *If your accident happened to me, I would be angry beyond belief and unable to see myself going on.*

I felt slapped in the face… I sat, alone, feeling as if I would never again find male companionship. It was horrible.

Emanating from somewhere deep inside me, I remembered these words from Bette Midler's song, *"The Rose"*:

> *"When the night has been too lonely, and the road has been too long.*
>
> *And you think that love is only for the lucky and the strong.*
>
> *Just remember in the winter far beneath the bitter snow lies the seed that with the sun's love in the spring becomes the rose."*

My former dance partner exited the stage and left me alone on the dance floor.

For a while, I was devastated. Besides Jeff's inability to see me as attractive anymore, I had been able to identify some of the feelings he created within me. This wasn't a bad thing, but at the time, I was struggling to not be angry, and to see myself as capable, worthy and desirable.

> *I was still a young woman, still a "Hot Girl," who had become a "Chick in a Chair" with the same feelings and desires for love and finding my man.*

My Own Home

I was excited and full of uncertainty. Yet, for the sake of my aging parents and for the quality of my own life, I knew it was necessary to become as independent as possible.

(Cousin Jean Marie Visits Katie, 1992)

*I*t was a big deal for me in January 1992, 15 months after the accident, when I was able to move out of my parents' home and into my own home.

There were two parts to this – finding a home that was wheelchair accessible; and also feeling able to live independently, to roll into this new life.

70

Wheelchair-accessible homes were very hard to find. We needed a place that was all on one level, without stairs.

My younger brother Tom searched the papers, the property listings and joined a property searching service. I found an ad in a small newspaper for a place that sounded perfect: a 900-square-foot, 3-bedroom, 2-bathroom home with a semi-finished walk out basement.

My Dad collected "donations" from my family to fund my independence. He didn't demand that anyone give. But he strongly suggested it, and most of my siblings did. Many of them gave generously. I'll always appreciate that.

My brother Bob, who was president of a national childcare center at the time, acquired one of the company vans with an extension that was no longer in use. Bob had the van painted for me. It was powder blue and beautiful. We called it "Big Blue." With the help of the State of Missouri, Vocational Rehabilitation financed the installation of a wheelchair lift.

My brother Tom and my college girlfriend Woody had fun driving this beast. Some of my caregivers were scared to sit behind the wheel but they eventually overcame their fear and we had so much fun coming and going.

Tom drove me over to the property in Big Blue, popped me up into the home -- and we loved it! The bathroom was tight, but aren't most? Tom moved into the house with me. I had the main floor, a tiny office and two small bedrooms. Tom lived in the finished basement and we shared the kitchen.

Soon after we moved in, one evening my aide had tucked me in bed when my old college friend Denise came by for a visit. My heart melted when she came to my bedside and said, "If I ever had kids, I would want them to spend time with you." That was nice to know, and it felt so good to have company at *my home*!

Paralyzed Problems

I'm not going to pretend that everything was great. Sometimes I'd roll by a flight of stairs, look down and think, *I could end it all, right here and now.* I'd hesitate for a second or two, then keep rolling, recognizing that I had already come such a long way from the day my life rolled over. I was growing in my mind and in spirit. I was learning to accept the physical changes in my body that I would never regain in this lifetime.

Independence also taught me to be more careful. There are so many frustrating incidents using a wheelchair. One day when I was alone, I inadvertently drove my chair under my computer desk and couldn't get out. I had to call my brother Joe and ask him to come over and get me out from under the desk. Joe was very gracious about it, but naturally he expressed concerns about my living alone when things like this could happen.

I've sat too close to a space heater and gotten a blister on my right arm that turned into a scar. I've injured my kneecaps by pulling up too close to a table. I've injured my toes and toenails by bumping into something which I never felt. I love to drink hot water but, on occasion, I have accidentally touched a full and burning hot cup without feeling the heat. Then I end up with a huge water blister that takes weeks to fully heal. These things are not a problem for people who "feel."

I quickly learned that living on my own had these hidden dangers.

But it was worth it!

Privacy was also an issue for me because those of us who use a wheelchair want privacy, just like everyone else.

Through Television, Leo Buscaglia Ignited A Spark

One night, I was in my bed, watching the public television network, and a special came on featuring Leo Buscaglia. An author and motivational speaker, he was known as, "Dr. Love." He was also a professor at the University of Southern California. Following the suicide of one of the students on campus, he noticed that many people felt disconnected and were searching for the "meaning of life." I didn't know all of this at the time. I just knew he was high energy, confident, bold, and had a unique quality unlike most "experts" featured on news programs back then.

Leo was genuine, forthcoming, and captivating. As he was speaking, something in me responded powerfully to who Leo Buscaglia was... not just what he said. He was being. He was a man inspired. He was taking to the airwaves to intentionally inspire others. He was unfazed by the fact that he was encouraging people to "connect" and "hug" back in the early 90s. He was the first to publicly suggest that we embrace those practices. Some probably thought he was impractical. I listened to what he was saying, and to what he was showing me. I liked his energy and from somewhere inside me came, *Katie, you could do something like that...* It was as if I was ignited – and knighted at the same time. I now had a true sense of what I was purposed to do...

Living independently has issues. Yet, it was necessary for my sanity and future to establish a place of my own – in my home, and in the world.

PART FOUR

Rolling On Purpose

We with disabilities, want to be known for what we can do, not for what we can't.

In those years, I was obsessed with showing the world my abilities, and afraid they would only see my disabilities.

I vowed to prove them wrong.

Defining Disabilities

The U.S. government defines disabilities as either
being physical or mental. But I believe there are
four types of disabilities: Physical; Sensory;
Cognitive and Psychiatric.
I have one in each of the four categories.

*D*isabilities, especially ones which are not easily seen by the eye, are often underrated in terms of impact, severity and treatment. Part of it is systematic, tied to the government's classification and cost, or to the insurance industry's ability to monetize. Another part is cultural, tied to our humanist nature of being private, embarrassed, in pain or simply uninformed about how (or if) we are affected by the disability. So, we function and learn to make the best with what we have.

Physical – How We Move

Spinal Cord Injury In My Neck at Cervical Five and Six

A ***paraplegic (para)*** *is paralyzed from the waist down often with use of their fingers. This is not set in stone, but most often a* ***quadriplegic (quad)*** *or* ***tetraplegic***, *like me, is paralyzed from the chest down, and while arms may move, fingers do not. The higher up the spine the injury* *is, the less you can do (less return to function). I do know of a fellow quad at my break level who can walk. The spinal cord nerves are made up of strands and his connections get through enough for him to walk but he must watch every step because he can't feel his feet. He often uses a wheelchair as a result. I had damage called "incomplete" because the spinal cord wasn't completely severed. My injury is incomplete because I have random feelings internally. A stomachache can mean indigestion, a bladder infection, the need to poop or female problems. I am grateful though, because a complete injury can damage your spinal cord so badly that no feeling gets through.*

Sensory – How We Touch/Feel

I Can't Feel 75% of My Body

All five of our senses can become disabled. Visual and hearing impairments are well known of by many. The parts that aren't working control other areas of the body for example, smell can be diminished in those who paint, have chemical sensitivity, have experienced chemotherapy and/or other medicines. These conditions can also affect the ability to taste.

Cognitive – How We Think/Process Information

I Have Adult Attention Deficit Hyperactive Disorder

In today's society these disabilities (ADHD, ADD, etc.) are often invisible and easy to hide until it comes to reading, writing and arithmetic. I think deep down, though much of humanity has attention issues. Today we have access to information on our cell phones, laptops and computers that process so much faster than when I grew up. No wonder our brains get distracted!

It wasn't until I was 51 years old that I got a diagnosis I should have had as a child: a person with Attention Deficit Hyperactivity Disorder

(ADHD). No one knows the cause of this condition or why it's three times more common in boys than in girls. But once I had a diagnosis, I felt so much less guilty about all the years I'd spent struggling to focus, distracted, impatient, and talking impulsively.

Psychiatric – How We Feel and Process Relationships with Ourselves and Others

I Experience Depression and Anxiety

Depression and Anxiety are *real* disabilities! I vacillate between them both so much it's like a game of ping pong. I mourn my loss and worry about my future. And please, don't tell me to "snap out of it." Instead, listen for a minute and then help me redirect my energy. Whenever I ask an audience, "Raise your hand if you know someone with depression and or anxiety," 90% of the hands are extended in the air. They are both extremely prominent today and run rampant in society.

Our health is worth taking care of and it's important to seek and maintain support in order to do so. Be your own biggest advocate by noticing and admitting if you're having difficulty in any area, and then seek what you need in order to take care of yourself.

Unfortunately, denial is one of the biggest obstacles to healing. We must change that.

My Singles Ad

After living independently for a while, I started to crave companionship. Reading the Riverfront Times Newspaper gave me an idea on how I could get back into the dating game.

*D*ating On Wheels required extreme measures, so I took out an ad in the newspaper!

I so wanted male companionship and I refused to give up.

My ad read:

> *"Petite, professional, outgoing, independent woman on wheels seeks male."*

I got over 30 letters in response to my ad! One of the letter-writers thought "on wheels" just meant that I drove around a lot! I could see that smooth communication with the "abled" was not always going to be easy. I tried to laugh about it. Another letter included a picture of a man standing in the woods with his shirt off. He scared the hell out of me.

After weeding through, I did go on two dates. One was to a movie with a guy whose letter had pictures of Groucho Marx all over it, but he was a boring guy in person. The second guy was a really, really nice man but I wasn't attracted to him at all.

***

Years later, while eating in a restaurant, a woman came up and asked me "Are you Katie?"

"Yes," I said. It was strange and awkward as I wondered how she knew me, and what she wanted to say.

"Well, a long time ago you went out on a date with my brother. He passed on this year, but he just thought the world of you." When she gave me his name, I recognized that it was that nice, nice man I'd gone out with once.

I offered her my condolences and wished her peace.

***

Taking out that ad showed me that I had choices, and that all choices weren't for me. It helped to build my confidence in a way; and it also showed me that I probably would not get the results I wanted through the newspaper.

As I continued sharpening my skills, I focused on being the best Katie I could be.

Reconnecting with Mrs. Schwartz

Finding Purpose... I think we are born with our purpose deeply rooted inside of us, and when we connect with it, what a difference we can make!

I had a ninth-grade teacher named Mrs. Schwartz. She had short gray hair and wore glasses. Precision was always her goal.

She had read an article about me, overcoming my accident, my advocacy work and my talks about disabilities in the *St. Louis Post-Dispatch* newspaper. One day she called and asked if she could come for a visit. It turned out she lived very near me.

I said, "That'd be great! Come over tomorrow."

She came over and brought me a bouquet of fresh flowers. We had fun talking about the past. She said, "One of the things I most remember about you was... you were quite the chatter box."

She had me there, and I had to laugh.

She told me how proud she was of me, her former student, using my experience, to positively inspire elementary school students. Before she left, she let me know that she was happy she had stopped by. She was glad I still had such a big, warm personality and that she would be in touch again.

Later, Mrs. Schwartz arranged for me to give a paid talk to the Kirkwood Retired Teachers Association. I looked out at the audience and recognized some of the teachers.

"Many of you used to tell me: 'Sit down and be quiet' Now, I'm always sitting, and sometimes I get paid to talk!"

The teachers laughed, and so did I. It was such fun. I recognized several of them though none were teachers who'd taught me personally. They warmly received me and acknowledged me for surviving what I have.

That day set me on track... I could be me, share my story, inspire others, be a chatter box AND earn a check? Heck, that was so much easier than the past few years, I wanted to do more!

Meeting President Clinton

*During his presidency, he was an advocate for
people with disabilities.*

I volunteered my time on many occasions with Paraquad, St. Louis' center for independent living. One of the things Paraquad does is to help people with disabilities lobby for their rights and wishes, just as any other American should be able to do. They asked me to come and speak to the Missouri House of Representatives and that is where and when I met Steve in 1993.

But in 1992, Democratic presidential candidate Bill Clinton was coming to Union Station in St. Louis, and someone at Paraquad called to ask if I wanted a ticket.

I said, "Of course," and it turned out I had a front row seat. When the (soon to be) President finished talking, he began moving along the front row, shaking hands. I was wearing my favorite black velvet hat, hoping to be noticed.

Suddenly, he was right in front of me. As he took my hand, I said, "Mr. Clinton, when you become President, please support programs that assist people with disabilities."

He said, in his Arkansas accent, "Bless you. And thank you for your suggestion."

I melted. The man had charisma. He was dripping with it. It matters not how you voted; Bill Clinton was a charming man.

During his tenure as President, the Clinton administration committed to providing $1.2 billion over five years, to the Work Incentives Improvement Act (WIIA) in 1999, which helped people with disabilities buy into Medicaid. They also committed to providing tax credits for work-related expenses for people with disabilities. Along with his Executive Order, hiring opportunities were expanded for people with psychiatric disabilities, and several other initiatives. I'm glad to know he heeded my suggestion!

Bill Clinton is not a bully. Not a fighter, but a lover and that,
I guess, contributed to his future political problems.

Don't I Know You?

It was odd that he seemed so familiar...

Through counseling, I worked on how I wanted to be. Active. I wanted to be active and involved somehow with young people. I wanted to educate people about what life is like with disabilities. I wanted to be confident and able to be assertive, but not conceited or bitchy and without a jealousy of people who have full use of their bodies.

Once I figured out what sort of person I wanted to be, I realized I wanted a different kind of man than I'd dated before. I needed someone deeper, willing to date "a chick in a chair," and more interested in political and social issues than any of my past boyfriends had been.

But in the back of my mind there was real doubt that I would ever find such a man. But the Universe puts you where you need to be.

I wanted to get involved in some political work on disabilities issues. I'd been a feminist since at least the 6th grade. Rights for those with a disability seemed like an extension of that.

In February of 1993, I was in Jefferson City, Missouri's capital, appealing to the House Appropriations Committee for funding that would allow people with disabilities to live in their own homes. We called it the Personal Care Attendant Program.

Politicians are used to these tradeoffs where you either spend more taxpayer money for better service, or you stave off tax increases in return for crappier government service. But the Personal Care Attendant Program gave those with disabilities better service for less money.

A slam dunk, right?

Actually, No. The problem was that it might look like a socialist program to a state senator who didn't realize how much money it was going to save the State of Missouri in nursing home costs.

I was determined to make the very best speech I could to the politicians gathered here. I was looking over some notes of mine when I saw a guy walking in my direction.

I stopped him and said, "Don't I know you?"

He shook his head and said, with a smile, "No."

Well, okay, but it felt like I'd known him forever. He was very polite, so I continued, "My name is Katie, and you are…?"

"Steve Banister, Program Manager for Services for Independent Living, the Columbia center for independent living, serving 20 mid-Missouri counties. I'm here training consumers on how to be self-advocates."

"That's cool," I said.

Then the Capitol staff called us into the hearing room, filled with a group of 15 politicians.

In my testimony I asked the committee:

"If you incurred a disability, where would you like to live?

Given a choice, one would innately answer: 'In my own home'....

"I ask you, ladies and gentlemen of this Appropriations Committee, look around this room full of people with disabilities. Not one of us invokes pity. Not one of us is ashamed by our existence. What we are ashamed of is government bodies who want to warehouse us in underfunded, dated institutions, often at an expense greater than our living independently in our community."

"Don't feel sorry for me. I fully accept my given circumstance. But you, today, who are gathered here have an opportunity to make lasting changes. Let me be the best I can. Help me to live as free a life as I can. Your funding of the Personal Care Attendant Program means I live independently, my caregiver has a job, and I can be a productive member of society."

When I was finished speaking, I knew I'd connected with the politicians because the room went totally quiet. It was so silent in there, it was freaky.

Then the committee chairman cleared his throat and said, "Katie, thank you for that most articulate presentation." Well, he was a politician. He had to say something like that. But the freaky silence that fell after I spoke cheered me up more than anything.

Then all of us had a little visit in the Governor's office with an aide to the Governor. Steve Banister was there, too. As I was preparing to leave with my attendant, Temia, I rolled over to Steve and asked him where he lived.

He said he lived in Columbia, Missouri, and then asked me, "Where do you live?"

I said, "St. Louis."

Steve smiled and said, "I grew up in St. Louis and my parents live in Manchester."

"Cool," I said. "Next time you're in St. Louis, look me up."

Steve was my age. He had a degree in Rehabilitation Psychology. Like me, he was committed to the idea that the state of Missouri has many citizens with disabilities, and a legal and moral obligation to meet their needs.

We talked about this and that, in an animated way. As Temia and I were leaving the state capitol building, Temia asked me what Steve and I had been talking about.

"Oh, nothing," I said.

"Well, I think he's kind of cute," said Temia.

Temia had long, gray-brown hair and good judgment. When she sized up people, she made very few mistakes.

I was thinking 'Shut up! Stop! I don't even know him,' but all I said was, "Yeah, but let's get me in the van and get going. I want to get back home."

The next day, Paraquad called me and asked me to go back to Jefferson City the next week, to testify in front of another committee.

I asked Temia if she was up for it. She said yes.

Then Temia said, "Why don't you call and see if Steve wants to join us for dinner when we're done."

I was taken aback, and I said no, Steve didn't even know me. The fact was, I didn't call men and ask them out. They called *me*.

(Persuasive Temia and Katie, 1993)

But my accident had changed so many things in my life. Maybe this was one more of those. Besides, Temia wouldn't stop bugging me. So, I picked up the phone. I'd barely finished dialing, when I heard Steve's friendly voice say, "Hello."

I put on my busy voice and talked fast. "Hi, Steve, this is Katie. Listen, I've got to be at the Capitol again next week and I was wondering if you'd like to join my attendant Temia and me for dinner afterwards?"

Steve agreed. We had a double date with Temia, and her fiancé. We had a great meal and lively conversation.

About a year after our meeting I wanted to go to Columbia to see him. Lanie was a paraplegic friend of mine who was looking for something to do and was a confident driver with hand controls.

I said, "Lanie, want to drive me to Columbia?"

She said, "Sure."

My afternoon attendant loaded me and my chair into Lanie's car and away we went – fast. We'd been driving 45 minutes on Highway 70 when the lights and sirens of a cop car came up behind us and pulled us over for speeding.

I looked at Lanie and said, "I hope he doesn't make either of us get out of the car!"

Living on purpose lead me to meeting my soul mate...

True Love

When the opportunity presented itself, I almost
chickened out!

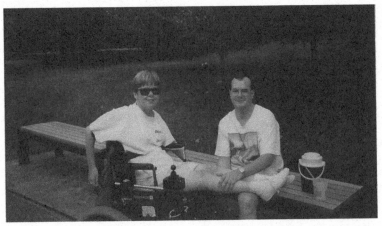

(Missouri Botanical Garden, 1995)

As soon as Steve expressed a romantic interest in me, out
came all my doubts. 'Oh, no, I can't date you. I don't do that
anymore. It's just not possible.'

*A*ny excuse would do, I was so doubtful. Plus, Steve had two
dogs and one of them did not like me. And, believe it or not,
her name was Katie! I hated that b*tch! She was a mean German

shepherd-Doberman mix, and she scared the hell out of me. Fortunately, I outlived her. The dogs stayed at Steve's parents' house while we were dating...

Steve reacted to my doubts in the best possible way. He didn't get angry or tell me I was wrong. But he didn't stop wooing me, either. Patient and gently persistent, he kept telling me I was beautiful.

Steve was very different from any of the men in my family. He was slow-moving, quiet, almost sedentary at times. He didn't have the need to be in constant motion like my father or brothers. He had a pleasant quality, a mildness, that was new to me, and that I truly would grow to enjoy and bask in.

He was very smart, and his mind was wide open to philosophy, ready to learn and grow every day.

Over the course of a year and a half, we became best friends, and I realized I was fighting off feelings of attraction. I drove Woody and my caregiver Temia crazy with my questions:

"Should I kiss Steve? Or not yet?"

"What if he doesn't like it?"

"What if I don't like it?"

"What if it ruins our friendship?"

Woody, having heard me over and over, in exhaustion yelled, "Kiss him!"

One day while Steve was over, washing vegetables in my kitchen, I said, "Pull up a chair and come sit by me." I looked into his eyes, held out my arms and we embraced. It was "Like buttah!" And we kissed – for an hour and a half.

Mind Over Bladder

As our relationship progressed, I realized Steve should probably learn how to help me with my personal care. To that point, I had never even let a male nurse attend to my very personal needs. The thought of Steve learning how to do my cath? It kind of freaked me out. I had hesitated about this, knowing that many people, men especially, are squeamish about bodily functions. Could I still be sexy to Steve if he was emptying my bladder?

I asked my overnight attendant, Lisa, if she would mind showing Steve how to empty my bladder. Lisa said, "Sure, no big deal." She laid me down, removed my pants, put my legs into position, and then went into the living room and returned with Steve.

Lisa cathed me and explained to Steve what she was doing. As Lisa removed the cath tube, Steve asked, "Is that it?" Lisa told him he had to keep everything sterile, and he nodded.

And that was it. My lover could cath me.

Being In Love

How can you tell if you're in love with someone? Lie down next to them. The feeling should be palpable. With Steve, it is.

One afternoon about a month later, Steve and I were together at a friend's summer wedding. The good old preacher was preaching, "If you love someone, you let them know it!" and I was sitting there listening to this and feeling the hots for my boyfriend.

Steve and I never made it to the reception. Instead, we went back to my place. I told Steve in no uncertain terms that I wanted to make love with him.

He started removing my tray, my foot pedals, my shoes…

I started crying and whispered, "What if this doesn't work, Steve? What if you're not satisfied? What if I can't do it?"

But soon when hugging him I could feel the pressure of his hands on my breasts. While committing the actual act, I could not feel him inside me, but it was more like a distant pressure, a tingling. Yes, my body is numb from the chest down, but I could enjoy his kisses on my neck and shoulders and soon it was, my God, oh, my God! It was lovemaking, it was the same beautiful feeling I'd had before -- but so much better because now I was giving my body to a man who was also my soul mate.

I'd been with my share of men, but this was by far the best sex of my life. For me it was all about emotion over physicality. Again, I can't really *feel* the act itself, but my body still works in the same way and I knew and still know that he can feel everything. And making him happy made me happy. It still does.

Steve is a very kind man. If he sees a bug in the house, Steve doesn't crush it with his finger. He gathers it in his hand, walks outside and releases it, reasoning that whatever pain and suffering you cause in this life, you're going to feel it in the next one.

Steve's father and mother were hesitant to meet me unless there was a formal announcement that Steve and I were engaged. Steve simply told them, "If you want to have dinner with me, you're going to meet her."

And that was it. Steve's parents caved. They met me over dinner and had to admit they liked me. I guess I wasn't their idea of what someone with disabilities would be like.

I love that Steve asks philosophical questions that make me think. Questions like: *"Why are we here?" "What are we here to do?"* And *"Do you realize how intertwined we all are?"* Questions like these have allowed me to ponder about the big picture, and to be more intentional and meaningful in day to day life.

> *Steve's love and his wisdom feel like a warm blanket protecting me from the storms of life.*
>
> *He is a great husband, and I absolutely love, cherish and adore him!*

You Can't Catch A Disability

Someone else's fear can paralyze others and
prevent enriching experiences. Practiced prejudices take away
opportunities. What a waste!

My sister Eileen drove me to give my first "Disability Aware-ness" presentation in 1991, a few months after I had gotten out of Rehab. Julia (my creative childhood friend) called me because her mother worked at a Catholic high school and wanted me to give a presentation to a group of her students.

I thought, *Why not?* It was raining buckets that day as Eileen loaded me and my wheelchair into her car. We were soaked, but we made it.

The students learned about *How It Feels To Be On Wheels*, living life with a disability. I could tell they were engaged and interested because they asked me some thought-provoking questions as well. That day I discovered that sharing my story not only helped educate others, but it was also therapeutic for me. Being an Inspirational Speaker and Disability Educator has helped me face and endure my life as a quadriplegic.

In 1994, I started getting more requests from schools to come visit as part of disability awareness programs. I hadn't advertised; I'd just given my speeches, and word had spread.

One conversation really struck me when a parent told me that they didn't want their children around people with disabilities, believing it would negatively affect them. I was livid. I wanted to cuss and fuss. Before I escalated the situation, I heard God telling me to chill out, so I went home and wrote a poem instead.

I don't believe that parent was trying to hurt me. The parent was trying to "protect" their children. Yet, I need all parents and people to know you can't catch a disability.

It's never been easy for me to deal with intolerant or insensitive people. Some stare at me. Sometimes I'll say, "Take a picture; it lasts longer." I wish people who stare at me would at least say "Hi" or "What's up?"

I am here in a paralyzed state to help others grow. That is *my* challenge. How others perceive me and treat me -- that is *their* challenge.

I want this sort of ignorance to die out, and the best way to do that is to help children and adults to understand what a disability means. Then we can have a society with more sympathy and understanding on this issue.

So ever since 1992, I've been doing appearances at schools, helping children to understand what having a disability means. I tell them that those with a disability may need their help, but no one wants to be treated like a baby. I tell them no matter what happens to them, not to sit around feeling sorry for themselves because there are surely other children who have it worse.

PART FIVE

Getting To the Wheel Truth

Some buried memories need to be uncovered and understood. Some worn-out feelings need to be let go, and forgiven... And some things are simply meant to be.

Scamming the System is Wrong – In 1990, the same year of my injury, the Americans with Disabilities Act (ADA) became law. It is a godsend to people with disabilities to help ensure entrance to public buildings and services with greater ease and dignity. I believe the ADA has been good for America, improved accessibility to state and local governments, non-profit agencies as well as public accommodations and commercial facilities.

In 1996, six years post injury, I was approached by a businessman who wanted to use me as a "secret shopper" to scout out non-compliant buildings in and around the Midwest. Also, he wanted me to testify against these businesses in court as an expert witness. He would then find a lawyer to begin mounting cases, a lot of cases as he put it. He also promised me I would be compensated greatly for my time. I immediately felt uneasy and forwarded the proposal to my local attorney. We agreed that more buildings should be fully ADA-compliant, but this was not the way to do it. I called the businessman back the next day and said, "No." I did not want to be a part of such a smarmy situation.

Joan's Visit

Lifting our previously unspoken burdens and finding peace in one night was an unexpected blessing.

One evening my dear childhood friend Joan came to dinner and brought her three teenagers, two girls and a boy. Everyone enjoyed the meal prepared by Steve. The young ones had so much energy, we loved it! As we were reminiscing about our school days, Joan said gently, "You know, Katie, I feel awful about what happened in sixth grade."

I knew what she was talking about and said, "Joan, bad things happen, and you did the best you could."

The kids looked bewildered. With silent confirmation from their mom, that it was okay, I began describing, in detail what had happened those many years ago...

What Happened

In 1976 when we were in the 6th grade, I felt free to be me and was friendly with all of my classmates. I had a variety of friends and we were always doing something. One evening Joan and I attended a movie night at Nipher, our school. I don't remember what the movie was, but it bored us, so we went in front of the school to hang out. It

101

was a beautiful night and with the steep hills we both agreed, "Let's roll down them!"

I rolled down and was laughing at the bottom when five boys on bikes rode towards me. Three of them jumped off their bikes and then jumped on me. I was wearing my favorite gingham yellow shirt that my mom hand-made with my name embroidered on it. The stretch top was being pulled in all directions exposing my bra and its contents. Yes, I had on a bra. I had boobs in 5th grade and started my cycle then as well. I was more physically developed than other girls in my class... Many lips were trying to kiss me. I was scared. Super scared, but I kicked and punched back ferociously screaming, "Get off me!" I think three of them took turns on top of me while two others stayed on their bikes and watched. To all of them, it seeded a fun game but to me it was, '*You can't do this! Not to me! Not today! Not ever!!!*'

After what seemed an hour but was actually a few minutes, the boys knew they weren't getting very far. They jumped back on their bikes and took off. I felt relieved and tired and stood up, seeing a paralyzed Joan. She had a look of concern as well as an, '*I didn't know what to do*' look across her face.

I tucked in my shirt and we walked silently back into the gym. The film was still going as I went over to the gym teacher and said softly, "I was just hurt by a group of boys."

He snapped back, "Well, you shouldn't have been out there!" and dismissed me. So I thought, *I'm glad it was over,* as Joan and I found a seat.

The next day, I was called to the principal's office to find my mother there too. She said, "Now Katie, one of your friend's mothers called to tell me something happened to you." The principal put a yearbook in front of me demanding, "Katie, identify the boys who harmed you."

Looking at the pictures I cried, "It was such a blur. I don't know any of their faces. I didn't know any of them!" After a few minutes the adults realized I wouldn't be able to pick them out. I didn't want to get the wrong people in trouble. That was just me, I wanted to move on.

By openly sharing with Joan's teenagers what had happened, not only did we have closure and healing, but we also demonstrated what true friendship, forgiveness and not holding grudges is all about. Dinner finished on a high note, and we ended the night with hugs all around.

***

In 2012, Joan got married for a second time, and I was thrilled when she asked me to officiate at her wedding. Together, Joan and I created a beautiful ceremony.

How did I become a minister? In 2007 an occupational therapy student whom I had become friends with asked me, "Katie, I love you and is there any way you could officiate my wedding?"

I thought, "Why not?" I investigated Missouri law and I learned that anyone could do this if they are affiliated with a church. I looked online, found the Universal Life Church and they ordained me for a fee.

I have performed five weddings and my mother's burial site ceremony. I love weddings and funerals. Those in attendance honor connection and letting go.

***

Joan's now adult children are still in my life and consider me the "cool aunt." I love that.

Today I can admit that I didn't really want to think about the incident after it happened. I had resolved it in the recesses of my mind and coped by not thinking of it. When attacks, especially of a sexual or violent nature happened back then, and even today, society tells us to shush, and that's not right.

I'm grateful for the #MeToo movement, yet I know we still have a long way to go.

Rodriguez vs. The Car Company Trial One

I was totally unprepared for the way they would try to classify me as a "party girl" who got what she deserved. But I knew I wouldn't and couldn't give up!

$\mathcal{I}$ don't like conflict. I would have preferred a mediation process with the Car Company. But it became clear very early in my recovery that I was going to have to file a lawsuit and get a settlement in order to live a normal and fully independent life.

On February 12, 1990, the day after injury, my family kicked into action. My brother Joe's wife Linda worked as a paralegal and set up meetings with three law firms in St. Louis. My brother Bob and Dad interviewed them and picked Hoffman & Wallach who were at the scene of the accident later that day. Our SWAT team of love thrives when needed and given a mission.

For one thing, I would need an aide for the rest of my life.

Let me say right up front that I don't begrudge these aides a good living; theirs is not an easy job. But the fact is, good attendant care is expensive, and costs will only go up as Steve ages and can't do as much for me.

Forget about buying a car or van off the lot; all of my vehicles would have to be specially adapted to my needs, with roofs raised, floors lowered, and a lift and lock-down system installed so that I could safely enter and exit and ride in the van. That process would cost me about $60,000 every time I bought a new vehicle.

Every five years or so, I would need a new $25,000 wheelchair and Medicare would only pay for part of it.

I would have chronically high doctor and dental bills, and an expensive array of medical drugs which I'd need to take daily.

It was also clear to me that I was not going to go after Delilah personally. Yes, she'd been the driver -- but she was a friend. I felt the vehicle was not a safe one, and that should be the focus, not Delilah's driving.

Still, I knew that taking legal action against the Car Company was going to involve Delilah. She was going to get deposed by my lawyers -- and by the car company's lawyers. She was going to have to relive the accident many times.

As I pursued my lawsuit, I stayed in touch with Delilah. The SUV manufacturer could not keep me from doing so. I had only known Delilah for six months before this mess, but she was a friend and a faithful visitor.

In 1995, I had my first court trial. I rolled into the courtroom in my chair and was… underwhelmed. It was just a plain old room with a couple of tables, and places for the judge and jury to sit. Courtrooms on TV were much more impressive. I guess I'd been spoiled by "L.A. Law."

There were more than 10 lawyers present, plus tons of legal assistants and mountains of paperwork. Everything that either side did was a tactic, an effort to gain the upper hand.

In time, this legal action became a circus. The arguing got ugly.

A lawyer in a court case is like the composer of a symphony who is also its conductor. The lawyer is introducing themes, lines of argument, just as a composer introduces musical themes. The lawyer's themes don't need to make literal sense, but they must "play well" and be in harmony with each other. Friendly witnesses are like the lawyer's musicians -- soloists playing and embroidering the major themes of the case under the lawyer's direction.

Meanwhile, the defense lawyers are constructing a completely different symphony with wildly different themes. No wonder the jury, as audience, gets confused! The jury is taking in two totally different productions, the one intercut with the other.

The lawyers for the Car Company took the offensive early on – a common defense lawyer tactic. Put the injured person on trial. Examine their life under a microscope and see how ugly you can make it look. The car company's lawyers painted me as a party girl who got what she deserved.

But now it was time for the other symphony to begin, my symphony, and its opening theme was – "Car Company, at what point in time did you lose your soul? Because you *knew* you had a defective SUV, but you sold it anyway!"

My lawyers knew that the Car Company would reply to that, "It's *not* defective! It's *not* defective!"

So, we had ready our second theme: 'Tell that to Katie Rodriguez! Look at this young lady and tell her there's nothing defective in your vehicle that rolled over on her, and whose seatbelt failed. Look her in the eye and tell her!'

But the car company's lawyers had a second theme ready, too, and I have to say it surprised me not only for its falsity but for its sheer gall.

Their second theme was: 'Katie's life is *better now than it was before the accident.*' What a steaming pile of crap! But that's what they argued. The lawyers for the car company insisted that because of all the wonderful medical care I'd gotten, and the great support I'd received from friends and family, I was better off paralyzed than I'd been before. What a twisted way to look at my life.

But I was afraid it might work. Corporate defense lawyers are very, very good at what they do. Get in the pool with them, and you are swimming with barracudas.

I'm limited in what I can say here about my own case, but it's well documented that people have died in rollovers by that Car Company, many have been injured, and the company has been sued many, many times on this one issue -- that this SUV model tends to roll over when it's turning.

I had a St. Louis lawyer named John, who had a casual manner, and a "prove-it-to-me" personality. Behind the façade, he was very, very competitive. But I guess to be a litigator, you'd probably have to be competitive.

John brought in a lawyer from Georgia named Jim, who had this wonderful southern accent. I'm telling you, if you ever need a lawyer for a jury trial, get a southern lawyer.

Jim's opening statement was: "Ladies and gentlemen of the jur-aaah, you have a wuuunderful oppoh-tunity hee-ya..." He was working the room like a rooster. He'd get up, take a step, tip his head to the side, blink his eyes; take another step, strut and pose, before taking his seat again.

He had a leg injury and used his cane not only to walk but to punctuate his words. The limp came and went, seeming more pronounced when the jury was in the room.

The lead attorney for the car company, George, was a short old man with wiry, close-cropped gray hair and a tough, crotchety manner. I tried not to hate the car company's lawyers. I knew they were totally oblivious to what it's like to be paralyzed. They didn't have a clue and they didn't care -- and I'm sure they still don't, unless they, or someone very close to them, has become as injured as I am.

I could see the trial was going to be a long and complicated one, but many of the potential jurors seemed very interested in it, and those eliminated from the jury pool often left the courtroom with a disappointed look on their faces.

One potential juror who looked about 55 was dismissed as a juror and he was pissed about it! He walked right by my wheelchair and gave me such an intense look of disapproval and disgust as he passed. I was ecstatic when *that* juror was eliminated! I got the feeling he wanted to side with the poor old car company, not this uppity young lady.

The jurors' eyes always seemed to be on me, and I felt some of them thought I was faking – that I wanted to win the case, get a huge payday out of it, and then ditch the wheelchair, walk to my car and go driving off, laughing all the way to the bank.

The way a lawsuit works, each side must present the other with a list of its witnesses. The Car Company's lawyers showed me their witness list and one of the people on it was Heather, my friend from early in high school.

I freaked. First, I thought: *What do they want to talk to her about? She didn't know me at all at the time of the accident.*

Then I thought: *Oh, my God, they wouldn't be using her as a witness unless they got something bad from her when they interviewed her. What would that be?*

Then I realized: *The rum and cokes! The little bit of rum I smuggled out of my house so Heather and I could make rum and cokes at our high school parties! That car company is going to take that little bit of my history and try to paint me as a big drinker who probably caused my own paralysis by being drunk.* It's crazy, not logical at all, but that's what my mind was doing watching this court case unfold in front of me.

I watched for days and then weeks as a parade of witnesses went by, and the case dragged on.

My high school principal was asked to testify on my behalf. He agreed, so long as I was not in the room. He was afraid he was going to cry.

I sat outside during his testimony. When he came out, he knelt down – and he was over six feet tall – and in his southern-inflected voice he told me, "Now, Katie, I told the jury what a fine young lady you were back in high school, and now as an adult."

I hugged him and said, "Thank you! I know you're a busy man, but I really appreciate your presence here today."

He replied, "Katie, I hope it helped. Now, don't you worry. This, too, shall pass."

Honestly, I don't think the lawyers for the Car Company wanted me in the courtroom at all. One day, I was stretching side to side in my wheelchair, after sitting still for hours. After the jury was sent out on break, one of the Car Company's lawyers said to the judge, "Your Honor, the plaintiff is calling attention to herself by moving back and forth in her wheelchair!"

He made it seem like I was a master manipulator.

One of my lawyers, Robert, responded, "Your Honor, Katie is only adjusting her body, which is stiff from sitting so still."

The judge looked at me. "Katie, you may stretch. But please do most of your stretching while the jury is out of sight."

I replied, "Thank you, Your Honor."

Heather was never brought to the stand to testify. I'll never know if she refused at the last minute out of some loyalty to me, or if the car company thought they had better ways of portraying me as a lush who'd gotten what she deserved.

But I'm grateful that I never had to watch my old friend being used against me.

My Mom would be there in court saying loudly, "I don't understand. What's going on?"

My lawyers told me, "You need to keep her quiet." Easier said than done.

Steve was still in Columbia. I gave him updates by phone, but I felt lonely. Steve was able to come occasionally.

One day, a lawyer for the Car Company was holding a piece of evidence, and my counsel, Robert, asked to see this piece of evidence. Opposing counsel threw the piece of evidence at Robert, and it hit him in the chest. Trying to physically intimidate him.

Robert quickly puffed himself up and said, "Suh! You ah no gentleman!"

The judge wasn't there, but the bailiff was, and he went and got the judge, who came hustling back into the room, reprimanded both lawyers and reminded them that she could hold them both in contempt of court, which would seriously damage their professional reputations.

There was no more throwing of objects at each other.

I'm not a shy person but sometimes I'm insecure. Each day I went to court with a 'Get-out-of-my-way' attitude. But when that day in court was over, I'd go home and cry, cry, cry.

Many people assume the media's pretty nice to you when you're paralyzed but that's not really the case. Many journalists portray those with disabilities as very weak people, who need our pity – and they think their sob stories are doing us a favor!

Then if someone with disabilities sues a big corporation like the Car Company, the media quickly flips the script. Now, we're not pitiful and weak. We're grasping and selfish – maybe even dangerous, because we're attacking the free enterprise system, which could cost the region jobs.

But I felt, in my case, the local media was fair. No complaints.

My Dad was very helpful to me in those difficult days. He gave me constant words of encouragement and kept me pumped up.

Then came the day when I took the stand. It was now on me. The chair where most witnesses sit had been removed to make room for my wheelchair. I drove my power wheelchair and parked at the witness stand. I felt ready, and I think I did well.

By the end of the case, I had come to the following conclusions about our legal system, or at least about cases like mine: It's a game. To you it may be a life-or-death issue but to your lawyers and to those on the other side, it's a game. It's also a waiting game, where each legal team watches the other for a mistake, so they can pounce.

It's a slow game, and it can be a demeaning game for the plaintiff and the defendant, if they allow it to be.

Court cases can bring out "the truth" – but a lot of people and other things can get exploited, or even ruined in the process. One thing that's lost in a court case is an edgy sense of humor like mine. It's too easy for the other side to use it against you.

I won the case at trial.

My lawyers then held a big, expensive celebratory dinner at the Adam's Mark hotel downtown, near the Arch and Busch Stadium. There was good steak at the dinner, and fine linens and pastries and an air of jubilation from our lawyers.

I love a good party anytime and was very happy that night.

But Steve was very solemn, almost angry – because he was convinced we were celebrating too soon. He knew the Car Company would appeal the case and felt we should celebrate only when we won the appeal.

I told Steve, "Will you stop it! We won the case, and I want to celebrate!"

The Car Company did appeal to the Missouri Supreme Court.

My lawyer Jim told me, "Don't worry. Even if the state's highest court doesn't like the law, they'll only change things going forward, for future cases."

But when the Missouri Supreme Court announced their decision, the justices decided to make the new law retroactive to my case, for the first time ever in Missouri history. My lawyers were chagrined but not very apologetic to have been proven wrong. It didn't make Steve feel any better that he was proven right.

I felt like someone who had just won the 100-yard-dash being told 'Oh, it's now a 200-yard dash, run it over again.' It just didn't seem fair. I played by the rules, did what was asked of me, and it sucked when they changed the rules.

The Second Trial

The Car Company changed their tactics this time around, attempting to paint me as some type of "Super Woman" who was better off, in my current state.

A month after my first trial, I was at the Green Tree Festival in Kirkwood Park, in my hometown of Kirkwood. It's a great event, always well-attended with tons of good things to eat. Every 10 feet I rolled, I seemed to bump into someone else I knew.

Then I heard a man's voice say "Katie, over here." It was a guy I knew, someone on the professional staff of the Recreation Department.

"Hey," I yelled. "What's up?"

In a snide way, he said: "Oh, Katie, we have a winery section this year. You ought to check it out."

Another jerk, having a little fun at my expense. Yes, he knew I was injured after visiting a winery. He said it to be mean.

I gave him an F.U. look and rolled on, but it hurt.

A few years after my first trial, I was in the parking lot of Union Station in downtown St. Louis when a tall, skinny young African-American man came up to me and asked: "Do you remember me?"

114

I answered, "No, sir, I'm sorry, I don't."

He said, "I was on your jury! I'm so glad you won your case! The lawyers on the other side, well, I didn't like them. And I wasn't the only one."

"I feel ya!"

He went on, "But your lawyer was good. He was *smooth*... just like Matlock and Denzel Washington!"

We shared a laugh, but the man was as mad as I was when I told him that there was going to be a second trial because the Missouri Supreme Court had overturned the verdict. I told the guy he wasn't the only one who was pissed!

Before he said goodbye, he told me: "You'll get them again. Any jury will see to it!"

But a trial is always very difficult on you, even if all the facts are on your side. You always have the sense that the other side is looking for every little weakness, any mistake that can allow them to win the case on a technicality.

On one trial day, I arrived at the downtown courthouse in Big Blue, my old van, and there, parked all over, were about 10 SUV's -- the same model I was in when my life was turned upside down. I had to laugh, as I entered the building, and got patted down by the security people. Ten of those SUV's... Were they trying to intimidate us?

Make us believe that this model was so popular that we could never win our case? Who knows? Weak people flaunt it, but in the long run, it only makes them look pathetic.

During the trial I felt I was being watched on so many different levels. I'd hear clicking noises on my phone line, as if my phone was being tapped. I'd mention it to my caller, and then say sarcastically: "Yeah,

Car Company, I'm walking around my house right now. I'm faking my paralysis in the courtroom!"

Once, when I was on the phone, I looked out the window and there was a car parked a little too close to my house, and a dude in the front seat. As soon as I mentioned it to my caller, the car sped away.

Can I prove that the car company's lawyers had hired someone to watch my house? No, I can't. Do I suspect they had? You're damn right, I do.

During the second trial, around July 1997, my brother Tom, Steve and I had a garage sale one day – just to stay busy, to vent some of my pent-up frustrations, clean up my house and get rid of old cooking wares, tchotchkes, clothing that no longer fit. It was just like anyone else who has a yard sale.

The Car Company sent someone to the garage sale… driving that same model SUV, naturally. The driver pulled into my driveway and made no attempt to buy anything. She just sat there, watching like a bully.

I shot her a mean look, and she pulled out and drove off. What possible legal advantage could the car company get from crashing my garage sale? Not much that I could see.

But they were sending me a message: *'We're watching you all the time, both inside the courtroom and outside, too.'* That's the kind of stuff bullies do.

Intimidation would not stop me.

Losing Dad

We had established a loving connection which would not have happened without the accident.

(My Dad, Joe Rodriguez)

 ad could never laugh at himself or stand to be the butt of a joke, but since he mellowed with age, he did allow himself and others to laugh about certain things – like his slipping off the roof twice

– which he would never have tolerated laughing about when we were all younger.

By the time Dad was in his 70's he was taking Coumadin, a blood thinner for blocked arteries, he suffered several heart attacks and he also had problems with asthma. By 1998, his body was wearing out, and it was painful for all of us to watch.

In his prime, dad had a recycling system called "refunding" he used by collecting labels from things like jellies, canned fruit and toilet tissue. Once he had enough labels, he would send them in for prizes. It wasn't until I was an adult that I realized how he was able to do so much with so little – as he was able to use these "prizes" to give his wife and children presents and necessities over the years. When we were young, I just thought he was collecting because he liked it, as an adult, I realized he did it because he needed the extra income. As his health declined, so did the refunding, until he stopped it all together.

One Thursday evening, Steve and I were driving over to see my Mom and Dad. Two streets from their home, an ambulance with sirens blaring raced past us, and I saw it turn right on Brownell Avenue. *Oh, my God!* I thought. *That's my parents' street.*

Sure enough, the ambulance and a fire engine were parked in front of my parents' house. I stayed in the van and Steve went inside. He came back and said, "Your Dad stopped breathing, but they have him on oxygen now."

Dad slipped into a coma and was dying.

That weekend, at Lake of the Ozarks, I was supposed to be honored by the Missouri Junior Jaycees as one of "Ten Outstanding Young Missourians." But how could I go and abandon my dying father?

When I told my brothers and sister I was going to skip the award ceremony, and stay by Dad's side, my brothers scolded me, "Do you know how mad Dad would be if you don't get your award?"

I rolled up to his motionless body in the ICU, hooked up to beeping machines. "Dad, if you want me to go, show me a sign."

When Dad moved his head, ever so slightly, I decided to go to the award ceremony.

On Friday evening, Steve and I left for the lake. Three hours later, we were settling in at the hotel. I called my brother's house to see how Dad was doing. Mom answered and said, "He's hanging on, Katie."

"Okay, I was just checking in." I could hear my family gathered, telling stories, laughing in the background and for a moment, wished I was there, too. As I hung up the phone and rolled over to Steve, I felt a little better, since I was with my best friend. He held me in his arms as I cried myself to sleep.

Stressed by the knowledge that my father was dying, I was exhausted, and my throat was sore. I drank nearly a bottle of cough syrup to get

(Steve and Katie, February 7, 1998)

119

through the evening. With Steve in his tux and I in a black sequined dress, the honorees took our seats to thunderous applause. At exactly 5pm, the host of the evening placed a beautiful golden medal around my neck. In that moment I was honored to be honored, and glad I made the trip.

After a video slide show we gave our speeches, and I dedicated my award to Dad, telling the crowd that Dad was fighting for his life. After all of the ceremonies and such, we got back to our room around 10 p.m. I saw a flashing light on the phone, and I called the front desk. They told me to call my mother. In my heart, I knew what that meant.

I called Mom and calmly Mom said, "Your father passed."

I asked, "What time did he pass?"

"At 5 p.m."

I freaked for a moment, and responded, "I'll be there as early as possible in the morning."

After hanging up the phone I thought about my parents' marriage, my Dad being gone at 76 years old, and my Mom sounding so strong during this time of loss. Thank goodness Steve was there to console me.

After stopping at home, we pulled into Mom's driveway early Sunday afternoon. Most of my siblings were there and I was happy we were now reunited. Everyone was busy being busy, making arrangements of all kinds, which I appreciated. I wanted everyone to feel better and I shared that I had a video tape to show them. Two months earlier I had interviewed Mom and Dad, who had revealed their life-memories. Over 70 years of living and over 52 years of marriage in two-and-a-half-hours.

We popped the videotape into the player and hit play when two of my brothers decided to go order the headstone instead of watching.

Though I had hoped to hold onto that tape for years to come, I was glad that it had been made, and could be shared. Before the video was over, the brothers were back and did watch the remaining portion with us and enjoyed it as well. I gave all my siblings a copy.

We arranged to have Dad's funeral procession drive by the Kirkwood Recycling Center, on the way to the cemetery, our father's favorite place in town.

I like to call death "transition" because it *is* a transition from life on earth to what is beyond. In many ways, I feel Dad is still with me. The Christmas after he transitioned, the whole family was gathered at my house. I was in my wheelchair with my back to the front door, my little nieces and nephews were running around, and then suddenly I felt a cold blast of air go right through me, colder than I had ever felt.

Imitating my father, I yelled, "You kids shut the goddamn door!"

When I turned and looked at the door, it was shut tight. I knew it was Dad. I felt his presence so powerfully and, as I shivered, I felt grateful.

*After Dad passed, my siblings and I did our best
to care for Mom. He did almost everything for her and left
big shoes to fill. When I think of him, I smile, and whenever I
get a whiff of Paul Sebastian aftershave,
I feel his presence reminding me of his love.*

Litigation Gives Way to Mediation

*(The Legal Team, Maurice Graham, George Fryhofer
III and John Wallach and Katie, 1999)*

I won the second trial but it too, was appealed. In fact, the Car Company had over 100 nitpicky appeal points, many of which seemed beyond unreasonable. For example, they complained about the way I adjusted myself in my wheelchair and about the facial expressions of my counsel when they addressed the judge or jury. The pettiness was unbelievable. The Car Company's appeal was rejected by the

Missouri Supreme Court. Thus, my case was sent back to the St. Louis presiding judge for a third trial.

In 1999, the presiding judge in the case had seen enough, and he ordered a final mediation to end the lawsuits. My brother Bob was extremely helpful during this period. He was in the room with me and Steve and my legal team.

I had the feeling that the head of my legal team didn't like or trust the head of the Car Company's legal team – and vice versa. Ego was prolonging this legal fight.

I remember a very old man, a retired judge, was assigned to iron out a compromise. I recall a lot of waiting and lunch being delivered twice. A day went by and then a second day – still nothing. On the third day, patience was thinning.

My brother Bob was with me, because Dad had passed the year before, and he wanted to be with me as I waited.

Bob grew tired of the legal tug of war, believing we were wasting our time. Eventually he stood up and said, "I want to meet with the Japanese representatives."

My lead attorney said in disbelief, "Oh, really?" He didn't see how that could help matters.

Bob, during his corporate executive tenure, had spent time internationally and had experience with many cultures and customs, as he had successfully negotiated many corporate deals.

I don't know what was said or done but I do know that Bob was very helpful in getting the two sides to settle. He was my big brother, the eldest son and I was his little sister, who needed help. I have to admit "Bob the God" pulled through for me, and I was so grateful.

Just getting to the settlement was such a milestone. My therapist, Karen, had told me, "This is the worst it will be." She was right about that and now it was over. Ironically, in 1995 the year of my first trial, the vehicle I had been injured in was no longer being marketed and sold in the United States. Consumer Reports evaluated SUVs in the 1980s and the results proved the problems plagued with the high center of gravity they had. Today's SUVs are lower and wider.

"How much money did you get, Katie?" asked my mother.

"Mom, I told you I signed a document that I won't tell anyone that."

"Katie, you can tell your mother!"

There it was again, that aspect of my mother which could be infuriating but also comforted me. *Family comes first.* She couldn't conceive of a little thing like a legally binding document coming in between herself and one of her children.

As much as I loved Mom, I couldn't tell her. She had loose lips and wouldn't be able to keep the secret.

Steve and I celebrated the end of the litigation with dinner at an Outback Steak House. Over dinner, we realized that, even with my lawyers taking 40% of the settlement, I would have enough money to cover my care for the rest of my life. I could pay back my family members for the money they'd advanced me over the past nine years. And I did; I paid back every penny.

I had wanted to marry Steve for years by this time...

The Proposal

*There had been so many ups and downs, twists and turns,
I was in need of stability.*

*I*n 1998, a month after my Dad transitioned, I had to put my loving companion Missy to sleep. Missy was my black and white cat who had comforted me after my wisdom teeth were removed, who lived with my parents during Rehab, and who had returned to me when I moved out on my own. She was my longest relationship, 17 years. The grief I experienced during this time was difficult to manage.

With my Dad's death, I really wasn't sure what was next. Steve walked through my door with a "different" smile on his face than usual. He respected and missed my Dad as well, so seeing him look "up" was refreshing.

As Steve approached me, instead of saying hello and giving me a hug, he pulled a ring box out of his pocket and then got down on bended knee and said, "Kathryn Claire, will you marry me?"

I loved surprises and this was a big one!!!

I was shocked, replying, "I don't know what to say!"

Steve asked me with a smile on his face, "Do you want me to take it back?"

I shouted, "No! Don't take it back!"

"Yes, Steve!" I blurted out, filled with a type of joy and glee I hadn't felt in many years.

He placed the ring on my finger, kissed me, and then we held each other for a long time, just basking in hopes of a bright future.

The timing of Steve's proposal was truly a Godsend. Not only was I going to marry my best-friend, the prospect of us spending the rest of our lives together really cheered me up! I knew that my Dad was smiling down on the both of us. And it felt good.

Finally, Steve said, "Katie, I went by your father's burial site and told him I was going to take care of you."

At that I cried fresh tears of joy.

***

I wanted to marry him the next day. However, we couldn't carry out a celebration just yet. We knew we had to prolong the engagement until my legal case was completely settled because Steve's income would have counted against my Social Security, Medicaid and Medicare benefits.

Our Wedding Day

Our wedding was on May 27, 2000. It was absolutely beautiful. We were surrounded by family and friends, with the memory of my Dad, very present in the room.

My eldest brother Bob escorted me down the aisle to the song
"Moon Shadow" by Cat Stevens.
"And if I ever lose my legs, I won't moan, and I won't beg.
And if I ever lose my legs, I won't have to walk no more."

ev. Deb Bourbon performed our ceremony at a beautiful hotel in Chesterfield, a suburb of St. Louis. Steve and I shared vows which we had written together. With the $25,000 I received from Delilah's car insurance company for my bodily injury, I was able to cover, completely, the cost of our wedding! We had a wedding party of 14, a guest list of 200, and a wonderful band led by the late, great St. Louis Legend Oliver Sain. We ate chicken and steak that night! Everybody seemed to enjoy the open bar and the dancing under our lovely white tent connected to the hotel. Holding the celebration in one place made it easy for me to take care of my personal care needs and not miss much.

The food was, as my dad would say, "Top drawer!" Our 3-tier cake of different flavors was beautiful and topped with a clay sculpture of us. It was great of me but not of Steve. But he didn't get mad, he took it in stride.

I danced with my high school principal and dear friends. We video-taped it all and it is still fun to watch. The whole day rocked and as the evening ended one of the band members said, "We hope we can play your 50th!"

During the after-party on our floor, I asked Woody and Delilah for assistance. I had received a beautiful white, long flowing gown at my wedding shower and wanted them to put me in it. They transferred me, cathed and donned me in my gown.

I thanked them and then said, "Please go get my man!"

Steve walked in and his eyes said, "Wow!"

I said, "I have to admit, I'm tired."

He sweetly responded, "Well, I really want to make love to you. I didn't on the night of my first marriage that didn't work out so well."

So of course, we did.

***

Steve and I have enjoyed a great sex life over the years. We know that requires *Communication and Creativity*. I think it also helps that coincidentally, we both share the same ruling planet – the Goddess of Love, Venus, in astrology. We like to think we were, "Made for each other."

I am married to the love of my life!

(Siblings Dennis, Joe, Bob, Pat, Tom, Eileen, Katie and our Mom, Claire)

(The Bridal party Debbie, Ellen, Sue, Eileen, Woody, Dave,
Bill, Kimo, Rich and Mark with the Bride and Groom)

Our Love Affair, In Steve's Words

Timing is everything.

Steve says:

I was a late bloomer in the world of dating. The first girl I dated in college, Ann, I eventually married. I was 23 and she was 20. I quickly learned this was a big mistake. The next three years were filled with uncertainty, frustration, and disillusionment. Ann left me for another man, and we divorced in 1991.

I focused on work after all that. I loved my job. I was an Independent Living Specialist (ILS) at a center for independent living in the middle of Missouri. I helped people with all different kinds of disabilities learn how to live independently, get signed up for eligible services and I assisted them and their families to cope with issues related to their disabilities and life situations. I think I was exceptionally good at my job and I enjoyed it.

Meeting Katie

In 1993, I met Katie at the state capitol in Jefferson City when she was there to give testimony to the House Appropriations Committee, and she was eloquently asking for funding for a new state Personal Care Attendant program—new funding, which was hard to attain. Katie's speech was heartfelt and inspiring. Most people with disabilities there to testify were nervous and gave halting, scared, short talks. Katie was a grand orator, and she swayed the staunch politicians and convinced them of the importance and savings of letting people with disabilities receive self-directed care in their own homes as opposed to more expensive nursing home care.

After the testimony was given, Katie was inspiring, beautiful, kind, and funny as we convened in the Governor's office with our group of 20+ advocates, I noticed that she seemed a little interested in me as a person, though I did not really have my hopes up. My self-esteem was low then.

The next day, at work, I got a call from Katie saying she was going to testify in Jefferson City again the next week. Then she said, "Would you like to have dinner with me, accompanied by my attendant Temia?

I said, "Sure."

We agreed to meet in Columbia after her second capitol visit. Temia's fiancé, Joe, lived in Columbia, joined us at 'Glen's Café', a wonderful Cajun restaurant in downtown. We all got along and had a really nice dinner.

The next weekend, I brought my dogs to see my parents in the Manchester area of St. Louis and I visited Katie as well. Since I had a chauffeur's license and Katie had an errand list, I drove her around town in her van and helped her check tasks off her list.

Initially, I would visit St. Louis once or twice a month to visit my parents and to visit Katie. On one visit, Katie and I went to the St. Louis Art Museum. It really felt like a date to me and I was nervous. I figured I had totally blown it with her when she asked me to get a medicine pill out of her backpack. My klutziness kicked in and I spilled all her pills all over the floor in the middle of the museum. I was embarrassed. Katie did not see it as a big deal. I gave her the pill she wanted and put the rest back in the container. We continued to tour the museum and particularly enjoyed the Henri Matisse exhibit.

Any time I visited St. Louis, I would make sure I could spend time with Katie. Her positive attitude was always infectious. Our friendship grew stronger, and my love for her grew quickly. Over time, I met some of Katie's siblings, her parents and many of her friends and I got along with just about everyone. I went to Katie's 29th birthday party and I had a blast.

I Was In Love

We met in February of 1993 and by November, I was head over heels in love with Katie. I told her over the phone that I loved her, and she **freaked out***, telling me she could not handle knowing that. She said she needed to process what I said and told me not to call her for a week. That was sheer hell for me.*

Katie called me after a week and told me she liked me, but she just wanted to be friends. Damn. I blew it. But I had to be honest, so I did what I had to do. I did sort of lose my grip on reality for a couple months.

The following week I met a girl through work, Kris, who seemed to share a mutual attraction. She worked with the Developmental Disability Council. We had a client in common in a smaller town outside of Columbia, so at that time we were seeing a lot of each other professionally. Kris was four years younger than me and we hung out with her friends some in Columbia, mostly at bars. We went to some movies together.

I was really in love with Katie, but in my temporary insanity, I really wanted a relationship. Kris was nice and cute, and we shared a love of similar musicians. One night, after drinks with her friends, we went back to her apartment to watch TV and we ended up kissing. Nice night. The next weekend, I took Kris for a Saturday drive to St. Louis to check out record stores and to see a movie at the Hi Pointe Theater near Forest Park. I put my arm around her as the lights dimmed and Kris politely pushed it away and said, "Sorry, but I really don't like being touched."

Bummer. We drove home, and it was just odd.

The following weekend, I had agreed to help Katie find a Christmas tree. Kris thought that was weird. Despite her pushing me away, I had made that promise to Katie before I had started going out with Kris, so in my mind, I was justified. I helped Katie, as a friend, though dying a slow death inside, while having fun all the same.

The next week, Kris and I went to the "Blue Note," a Columbia night club to see the band "Counting Crows." As we were chatting before the show started, I told her about my tree hunt with Katie and Kris said, "Are you aware that you talk about Katie a lot? I don't think you are over her at all and I don't want to date you anymore."

And she left.

I watched the show with Eddie, my friend from the bar, and pondered my life.

During that concert I resigned myself to being Katie's friend. I continued to visit St. Louis once or twice monthly. Being close to her was so much better than the torture of her missing from my life. We hung out, did fun things and we continued to develop our friendship.

One day in late Fall we were chilling out at Katie's house, when her mom Claire, came by to catheterize her. Claire asked me if I could help her transfer Katie from the wheelchair to the bed since Katie's dad, Joe was not there. Of course I was willing, however, I looked to Katie. She nodded in approval of my assistance, so I put my arms under her armpits while Claire picked up Katie's legs. We did a successful two-person lift.

I left the room and Claire helped Katie empty her bladder. Once done, Claire called me back in and we transferred Katie back into her wheelchair. I knew we were friends, but it felt good, like a hug.

We spent that Christmas of 1993 with our respective families. I visited my sister Sue in Daytona Beach, Florida, and along with her roommates, we drove south to Key West, having an enjoyable time.

A New Year

I was visiting Katie in January 1994, and we were in her kitchen talking. I was cleaning fruit for us in the sink, chatting with Katie who was sitting behind me.

Katie stopped me, saying, "Pull a chair over here next to me so we can talk eye to eye."

I turned the water off and did as she suggested. She said, "I really want you to hold and kiss me."

I said, "Really...are you sure?"

Katie replied, "Yes, really. Kiss me."

I put my arm around her and with a big smile on my face, I touched my lips to hers. There was electricity and magic and fireworks as I sent her all my love.

We continued kissing for over an hour and a half.

Our lips were made for each other. Her body felt like perfection in my arms. I am not sure why the kiss ended; maybe my arm fell asleep or my lips were numb? The best thing was that I now knew that Katie liked me A LOT! It was official. We agreed that we were now dating.

Katie's sister Eileen and brother in law, Bill, had invited me to attend their son Dan's baptism. So, I went to Katie's house and joined her and her younger brother Tom on the trip to the church. Tom drove Katie's van

'Big Blue' and we joked and laughed on our trip. After the service, we went back to their house. It all felt natural to me, being there with Katie's mom and dad as well as siblings and their families. Everyone was welcoming and friendly, especially Katie's dad, Joe who liked my disability background and my interest in Katie.

Mutual Attraction

After that, I started coming to St Louis a lot more often, 2 to 3 weekends a month. Every time I visited Katie, we held hands, hugged, and kissed. And we talked on the phone every day, often more than once. I was able to love her now and it felt awesome.

In April of 1994 we decided when attending a friend's wedding ceremony, we wanted to progress our relationship by making love. To do this, I had to know how to take care of Katie's body. Katie had her attendant, Lisa, show me how her catheter procedure was performed. I watched and I got it (I had helped several men catheterize at my job and the concept was similar.)

Once our intimate connection took off, Katie was able to accept the fact that I loved her, and she was able to handle it when I told her so.

Over time, I took on more of Katie's care giver roles such as catheterizations, transfers, showers, bowel care, as well as shopping, meal prep and driving her van. I have always enjoyed helping her. Our friendship grew and developed. We had become best friends and then, lovers. I visited Katie every weekend. In 2000, I married my best friend.

***

Katie and I are a great team. Living and running Access-4-All together, really works for us. I love our mission to educate, empower and entertain. After twenty years of marriage and twenty-seven years together I continue loving my exciting, cute, and wonderful wife.

Getting Close To Steve Wasn't Easy For Me

There are reasons for everything...

After reading Steve's perspective of our relationship, you may be wondering, "Katie, why did it take you so long to let Steve get close?"

I had never let any guy I was with get too close because I thought it put me in charge and I liked holding all the cards. I slowed down for no one.

Early on as a young woman, I equated love as a physical exchange. I learned that if I took a guy's hand and let him walk with me, it made him happy. Affection got me attention, and I was there for it. Moreover, because of my very feminine physique I was a magnet of enticement and I used that, to get what I wanted, making me happy.

However, more than half the time, the 'spark' faded and I was left disappointed and alone. So, I was twenty-five and gave up on finding true love. It was not to be for me, not because I didn't want it, but because I didn't believe I would have it.

After paralysis I craved companionship, but unable to wear my form fitting white sweater dress and heels, I felt my magnetism lost its charge.

As you now know, it took all types of therapy to assist me in living in my "new body" and also to get comfortable and feel feminine again. Between the PT, the OT and the counseling, I had gained real self-confidence once I decided I wanted to live, and have a life worth living. For a period of time, though I had desire for companionship, my focus wasn't going out to bars, it was on being the best Katie I could be. I had matured and evolved quite a bit, through the accident and the experiences that came after it. I had begun to know myself and face my own realities. Some were sobering, however, I chose optimism whenever I could.

When I met Steve I was twenty-seven and he's six months older than me. He was nice, and I was interested in him, but it was psychologically safer to be present with him at a distance. Because when I met Steve I was at a relationship rock bottom. I had never had a successful relationship to that point, so close to 30 years old.

And I was too vulnerable to take a chance at heartbreak, from my wheelchair, with all the other things happening in my life.

However, I did not count on Steve's persistence. Over time I showed him the sides of me that scared off other men, but not Steve. I had had empty relationships. Prior to Steve, I lied to every guy I dated. I mislead them by making them believe I was having a relationship with them while I was likely working on a relationship with another guy. I thought I was in control, but I wasn't. The funny thing is, I didn't get caught in my lies very often, so I got away with them. I didn't think they were a big deal at the time, but they were - misleading meant that I acted, and went along with whatever suited them or me at the moment, which included sex, when I was younger. This behavior came out when I was bored or mad - I would be mean, irrational, make excuses and I drove them away when I didn't feel I had the control that I craved; or when I faced up to the fact that I couldn't control them.

Steve actually cared about my thoughts, my mind and eventually, being intimate in a way that completely satisfied us both. I finally realized that friendship was much more important than quick sex, superficial interactions or simple fun. Once I got to know him, and he got to know me, I could see that he could handle all of my emotions, outbursts, and feelings. I could not lie to him, and I didn't feel the need to even try. And that my tears did not make him uncomfortable? I had a winner. He enjoyed hearing my thoughts, deep thoughts and I loved hearing his.

Steve's fortitude and deep love for me equipped him in a way that I liken to the old carnival game, "Whack-A-Mole." Whatever I threw at him he never gave up. He still called and wanted to see me. He knows my mistakes and all the things about me that I don't like about myself and is still lovingly by my side. He proves his strength daily, assuring my comfort and safety, telling me how lucky he is to be with me.

Steve showed up at the right time, right place and after a year and a half, I completely let down my guard and knew we created the right everything...

Karen, My Therapist

We must remain open and willing to listen. Those are skills I learned in therapy with Karen.

By 2007 Karen and I had worked for about 18 years together. After my accident, she had come to my house for my sessions, knowing the traveling was easier for her than for me in my wheelchair.

But by 2007 Karen told me that she felt I didn't need her counseling anymore. I resisted this; I felt I still needed her.

She said, "Katie, when you came to me, you didn't yet know how to mourn. Mourning is one of the very most important things that human beings ever do, and you didn't know how. But now you do."

Gently but firmly, she let me know that, even if I was sure I still needed a therapist, I would have to find another one. Karen was trying to wind down her practice.

I knew I was a lot to put up with - but I hated to think I was driving a good therapist into retirement. After 18 years, I had drawn Karen into the very inner circle of my life. I cared deeply for her and relied on her.

It felt as though she were divorcing me. That wasn't her intention, but our last goodbye really hurt.

I was both dependent and empowered during therapy. There was a certain amount of comfort I counted on; yet there was a part of me that knew we wouldn't stay together.

I hated letting go, because it meant I had excelled and could process my feelings on my own.

We spent our last two months together discussing how my life was going. It was great; my life and the therapy.

Even now, when thinking of Karen, I feel mixed up. I could bawl. I miss her, I love therapy, I like taking the time to face my feelings, as long as I spit it out, it's okay.

She knew me before my accident – both versions of me. But it was time for her to retire. She was amazing, came to the hospital, helped psychologically, and she even came to my house for sessions.

The process of therapy was made harder with my injuries, yet with her support, I grew. Karen empowered me to be as strong as I was, living in this chair and she helped me understand my family issues.

I didn't want my therapy to end with Karen. I had lost so much already, and I didn't want to lose her. I didn't feel like I could make it without her. She felt that she had done all she could with me, I didn't feel the same way. Losing her was difficult and meant that I was more dependent on myself to process my feelings, and that scared the hell out of me.

Over time, I decided it had been a mistake to see Karen as a good friend. It was unfair to both of us, and to her most of all. She was a gifted professional, and in order to help me heal, she had asked permission to play some of the roles that a good friend might play. I had given her that permission.

I thought back to a day when I bumped into Karen, quite by accident, in a shoe store. She was with one of her children, I think. But when

I greeted her like an old friend, she barely acknowledged me. By her choice, there was no communication between us that day. If she'd really been a friend, she would have rejoiced to meet me in a shoe store, outside of the formal therapy relationship. But that would have crossed a line that Karen wanted no client of hers to cross. It was at that time, I realized we could never be friends – it was a professional relationship.

I've thought a lot about therapy, its uses and its drawbacks. It can certainly be mind-expanding, and it's saved countless people from misery or even suicide. But there's a downside to therapy, too, a tendency to become obsessed with yourself, and your own losses.

Over the years, I've worked with other counselors and a life coach to keep me on track. Knowing how and when to ask for help is one of the best ways to be healthy.

Meeting Ross Again

Closure is not always easy, but it is necessary.

One day in 2015, Steve and I bumped into my one-time almost husband Ross when we were in a parking lot. I was rolling out of my van when I heard a familiar voice say, "Katherine Claire Rodriguez!" It was Ross, my first love.

In 2004, I had mailed him a copy of my first book, *Aunt Katie's Visit,* along with a note apologizing for the way I had mistreated him. I let him know how happy I was, chair and all. He called me to thank me for the book. Ironically, his daughter had been in the audience at one of my elementary school talks shortly before he had received the book. He said she was quite taken with me and that made me smile.

I was physically very different from the Katie Ross had dated in 1982. Fortunately, I felt great about the way I looked that day. So, when I saw him in this parking lot, I didn't have time to dig up the dreaded idea of meeting him in person again.

He looked pretty much the same, still handsome, and in great shape.

We gave each other a big, sincere hug that allowed us both to have a genuine conversation, despite the past.

142

He shook Steve's hand and they acknowledged one another. He then told Steve he was lucky to be my husband. Steve agreed with him. I sat, smiling.

"How have you been, Katie?"

That's always a hard question for me to answer. I said, "Life has been… interesting."

"I heard about your litigation," he said.

I asked about his family and he asked about mine.

After some chit-chat, I was able to say: "Ross, I'm sorry about what happened between us. I was really crappy to you – and I'm sorry."

Ross and I had been very close when I was 18 and he was 20 years old. So close in fact, that he had given me a ring. At the time, I thought it was meant to be an engagement ring. However, on my graduation night, just before seeing my dad, he asked me to remove it. He didn't want my Dad to know he had given it to me. That hurt.

We continued to date after that, but in my pain, I cheated on him and then lied about it. Needless to say, after a bit more drama, I broke it off and had never apologized, face to face.

When I did apologize, in that parking lot, decades later, if felt good to acknowledge what I had done as a teenager, and to be over that part of my life.

PART SIX

Rockin' n Rollin'

Soul Role
We do not have a soul
We are a soul
Who embodies a body
So many souls wait for a human suit
Taking what they can get
But only for the opportunity
To be here.
Why?

A body feels the warmth of the sun
Gazes on earth's beauty and difficulty
Listens to the millions of life's reverberations
Inhales the earth, its people and baking bread
Though I can pass on passing gas
The crown jewel for me is taste
From a scoop of mint-chip ice cream

On A Roll

to a gooey warm grilled cheese

Oh, the opportunities
And after?
When it is our time to go
We check in for a review with God
Then again, we are souls
Waiting for a suitcase
And another ride

Life Is Not Easy

Everyone has to get up each day and make something of herself or himself.

Living life on planet Earth creates situations that are not always easy to deal with. Maybe you have problems at work, home, or at school. Maybe you don't like the person you are. You might wish you had a different life. Maybe you are mad and you don't even know why. How do I know these things?

Because I've felt this way, too! I have a lot of problems. But you know what? So does everyone. I know a lot of people want to be rich and famous. But rich and famous folks have problems too, albeit different than most. They lose their privacy. They have mega amounts of pressure to look good. I've read that people with fame and fortune have a hard time knowing who their true friends are. That doesn't sound very easy to me.

You might be battling depression, anxiety, learning disabilities, an eating disorder or problems believing in yourself. Yet, if you've ever thought about changing places with someone, think about the things you have going for you. Don't let the challenges be the focus of your life, let them fuel your determination to be hopeful. Everyone has to get up each day and make something of herself or himself.

Shift your focus and focus on what you want (more positivity) and start to let go of what you don't want (negative thoughts, feelings and actions that are holding you back).

Katie's List to Live By

1. You are not alone.

2. Sometimes the first move is the hardest. Make it anyway.

3. Don't give up, no matter what! Seriously.

4. There are ways to overcome ANYTHING.

5. Learn to appreciate what you do have (going for you). Doing so resets your thinking and allows gratitude to permeate your life and experiences.

6. Forgiveness is necessary to get over the past. That forgiveness needs to include forgiving others and yourself. Forgive.

How do I know these things?
I am living proof, and you can be too!

My Life's Work

*Children ask the darndest questions, and they get
to the heart of the matter.*

I think *when* we are born gives us a little insight to some of our characteristics and uniqueness. While nothing is written in stone, I enjoy learning about my own, and others' astrological signs and birth charts. I find it interesting and helpful when it comes to building relationships. That being said, I'm a true Libra and I love to share. We crave harmony and peace and want everyone to get along. However, my rising sign is Aries and that part of me wants everything done immediately. What this means is that there's a war inside me all the time. I want harmony, now!

When giving a presentation I talk about disabilities and let others know that having a disability isn't an end, but the beginning of something different. It takes time and effort to accept this, and live it daily, but it's my life. I also address about the importance of having a positive attitude and how I deal with it all.

The presentations with children are often the liveliest, as they don't mind asking questions after I've given my speech... they are often quite inquisitive after I demonstrate using my eating brace, my writing brace and my tenodesis brace that helps me put on my makeup.

149

These are the kinds of questions kids ask:

> *"If we cut your leg off, would you feel it?"*
>
> *"How does it really feel to use a wheelchair?"*
>
> *"Do other people make fun of you?"*
>
> *"What's your favorite color, food or TV show?"*
>
> *"Do you have to take a lot of medicine?"*
>
> *"How do you swim?"*
>
> *"How do you fly in a plane?"*
>
> *"Who cleans your glasses?"*
>
> *"Can you brush your hair?"*
>
> *"How do you put on jewelry?"*
>
> *"Could you have children?"*
>
> *"What happens if you get diarrhea or throw up?"*

I try to answer every question fully and openly.

When I answer a question about my bodily functions, some of the children will roll their eyes, others will put their hands to their face or turn red as a tomato, from embarrassment. I would have too, at their age. But I feel they should grow up knowing about how disabilities can affect us all.

I also try to have a sense of humor about it all. When kids ask me how I take a shower, I tell them it's like being in a car wash.

One 7th grader said, "I didn't think I should ask about someone's disabilities. I thought it would hurt their feelings. Is that true?"

I explained that everyone is different, and some people with disabilities will answer and some may not, and then gave her a suggestion.

"You could say something like, 'I don't know much about disabilities, but can I ask you about yours?'"

***

Ask for what you want and get the help you need.

I encourage kids to talk with their school counselor when they are going through tough times. I let them know that keeping their problems inside can be dangerous, causing aches in stomachs, heads or worse. During a talk at a St. Louis County middle school I said, "If someone is doing something that you know isn't right, talk to someone."

The following week the news reported that the principal at that school had been fired for inappropriate conduct with a student that had been in my audience. I was saddened that a person who is supposed to be "trusted" was not trustworthy, but I was also encouraged that these children felt safe and empowered to speak up for themselves.

I want everyone, including you to know that if you need a listening ear, ask for it.
You are worth taking care of!

Finding Humor

Some things are actually funny, and others, are not. I've learned to find the humor in certain situations, just to get through the tough days.

Scotch and Tape

Funny things happen to you when you're in a wheelchair, just because people aren't used to dealing with someone in your position. Once, at an Asian restaurant, I realized I'd forgotten to bring my eating brace.

But I figured at least we could tape my fork to my hand, and I asked the waitress if she could bring some Scotch Tape with our shrimp and pea pods.

When she brought me a shot of scotch I laughed! Realizing there must have been a language barrier, I told her, "That might make the ride more fun, but it won't help me eat."

We all had a full belly laugh at that, we cleared everything up…

She returned with tape, and Steve taped my fork to my hand. The meal was delicious and I laughed at myself later, realizing that "Scotch" tape was a brand name anyway. So both of us had a "use of" language barrier.

Mom and Medicine

While no disability is "funny" or "humorous," I've learned to use laughter to replace tears, as a way of coping. It's also important to find the light side of serious situations. I was watching TV with my then 80-year-old mother one evening when a commercial for an antidepressant came on and we had the following conversation:

"I'm glad I don't take medicine like that."

I calmly responded, "But ma, you do take that medicine."

In her proud voice laced with utter disgust she questioned, "Now, why would I need such a thing?"

"Mom, because you're being a bitch when you don't."

"Well!" was her only response.

I chuckled under my breath. I still respected her but sadly, the truth is the truth.

Doctor and Lump

Once, when I was on the operating table for a lump in my left breast, my well-qualified doctor looked down at me 15 minutes into his work and said, "Ma'am, you're one of the stillest patients I've ever worked on. You haven't moved an inch!"

I said, "Doc, you do know that I'm a quadriplegic, paralyzed from the chest down?"

He said, "Oh, yeah" and went back to work.

For a doctor to be that clueless is either outrageous, or it's funny, and I choose to find it funny.

So, I use humor to help me find peace.

Managing vs. Muddling

Denial, Anger, Bargaining and Depression are the first parts of the 'Five Stages of Grief' remember that - so you can get to the fifth step, Acceptance!

I discovered that there were *Five Stages of Grief* through watching an episode of The Simpsons television show! Homer possibly ate the venom of a blow fish at an Asian restaurant and his doctor gave him 24 hours to live. Homer responds:

Denial   "No way, cause I'm not dying"

Anger   "Why you little…!"

Bargaining   "Fear? What's after fear doc?"

Depression   "Doc, you gotta get me out of this; I'll make it worth your while."

Acceptance   "Well, we all gotta go sometime."

It's kind of ironic that the cartoon has lasted so many years, and that it's turned out to be so relevant in certain ways, to real life. If you think about it, we've probably had many "five stage" experiences. Recognizing them is the first step to getting through and past them.

Elisabeth Kübler-Ross and David Kessler research - The five stages, denial, anger, bargaining, depression and acceptance are a part of the framework that makes up our learning to live with the one we lost. They are tools to help us frame and identify what we may be feeling. But they are not stops on some linear timeline in grief. Knowing this not only cleared my mind, but also seemed to free my soul. Also, understanding that it's not just a line – but a continual process – dealing with grief, gives me relief whenever I need it – and this can happen several times, daily.

Honesty, within Me

When I share my honest feelings and how things really are, it helps me with acceptance and can be a lesson for others to learn from. Prior to writing this book, I had a fear of speaking to adult audiences. I was much more comfortable speaking to children, or at least those younger than me. As I began to process what was happening, I realize I had been stuck in various forms of grief and denial based on being the 6th of seven children, and also on my experiences, in my chair. However, I decided to use my methods (those learned from others and those I developed to cope) in order to conquer the issue.

My self-talk before speaking in front of adult audience at a Synagogue was:

- I am just as worthy as someone older than me; and my experiences are just as valid as a tool for others to learn from.
- People often ask, "Are you mad at God?" No, I'm not. I tell them, "God didn't do it, God gets me through it."
- I wake up with a good attitude and deal with my depression … and yes, if I'm an inspiration for others, I'll be that and am happy to claim it.

- My acceptance has affected my being and has also opened the doors for healthier and better relationships.
- Awareness brings about a choice/brings about the ability to choose.

I focused on my intention, inspiring my audiences, not impressing them. Being an Inspirational Speaker versus a Motivational Speaker... Motivation is usually incentive based... Ra rah! However, Inspiration comes from inside. Inspiration is about tapping into that inner connection where we are sharing our truth - happy, sad, angry or excited; in a way that someone else may or may not choose to connect and be affected by that inspiration. Through sharing, the opportunity is there. **Inspiration can feed your soul, fuel your mission and prepare you for your purpose.**

Think about your life and issues you may need to face. You can get through them, with awareness, support and the willingness to get beyond previous results!

Katie's Inspirational Mantras for Daily Living:

1. I don't want to be angry as a practice – I choose to practice Acceptance.
2. Therapy for my mind and body is a priority, and I choose healthy practices daily.
3. Hope and fun are important to me, and I live to experience them, each day!
4. I understand my life as it is today, and I commit to making the most out of what I have been given, body, mind, soul and experience.
5. I choose each day to stop living in the past – I allow my present to unfold in forgiveness and kindness, knowing each thought and feeling starts and ends with me.

6. I choose to find peace with my past and those who may have wronged me knowing that the more I let go, the more joyful I become.
7. I trust in God.

Choose appreciation daily... email, text, call, or better yet, visit those who are important to you – and hug yourself every single day, you deserve it.

About the Author

Katie Rodriguez Banister is an inspirational speaker and disability educator. Since the accident that left her a quadriplegic, she travels with her husband Steve teaching self-awareness and acceptance. She's presented to thousands of children and adults around the country– demonstrating how to ward off anger, finding beauty in the bad.

Also by Katie Rodriguez Banister:

Books

Aunt Katie's Visit

The Personal Care Attendant Guide (Demos Publishing)

A Pocket of Poems and How to Write Your Own

Karmic Validations

Music & Poetry

Beauty in the Lou